List of Contents

Prologue: A Guide to Introverted Success

In the bustling field of success, the voices of the extroverts boom like vibrant hawkers, their achievements glittering like polished gems on display. Their paths are paved with bold pronouncements and confident strides, their victories celebrated in the dazzling glare of the spotlight. But amidst this clamor, a quieter path unfolds, a path for those who find their strength in the whispers, their wisdom in the shadows, their victories in the quiet hum of introspection. This is the path of the introvert, a path where success is not a trophy hoisted for all to see, An intricate interplay of self-discovery, quiet resilience, and the steadfast pursuit of personal fulfillment

For centuries, the introverted story has been shrouded in misunderstanding. We've been painted as shy wallflowers, anti-social loners, or even lacking in ambition. Our quiet contemplation mistaken for social awkwardness, our preference for solitude misconstrued as indifference. But within this quietude lies a vibrant power, a reservoir of untapped potential waiting to be unleashed. We are the deep thinkers, the insightful observers, the architects of meticulous plans and the creators of profound ideas. We are the loyal friends, the empathetic listeners, the champions of genuine connection in a world obsessed with fleeting interactions.

This book is not a call to conform to the extroverted ideal, a guide to mask your introverted nature or apologize for your quiet strength. It is a celebration of your unique path, a map to navigate the hidden terrain of introverted success, and a torch to illuminate the power that lies within. We will delve into the myths and misconceptions that have held us back, shedding light on the true nature of introversion and its inherent strengths. We will explore strategies for navigating the challenges of a world built for extroverts, from navigating social situations to thriving in demanding careers. We will celebrate the joys of introverted living, the power of solitude, the beauty of meaningful connections, and the quiet satisfaction of personal growth.

But most importantly, this book is a call to action. It is a call to embrace your introverted self, to reclaim your narrative, and to rewrite the definition of success on your own terms. It is about recognizing that your introversion is not a weakness, but a superpower waiting to be activated. It is about understanding that your quiet voice deserves to be heard, your thoughtful observations valued, and your unique contributions celebrated.

This path to success won't be without its challenges. You will encounter moments of doubt, whispers of insecurity, and situations that demand you step outside your comfort zone. But within these challenges lie opportunities for growth, for pushing your boundaries, and for discovering the depths of your own resilience. Remember, the quietest trees often bear the sweetest fruit, and the most profound journeys often begin with a single, silent step.

So, dear reader, if you find yourself drawn to this path, if the whispers of introverted success resonate within you, then let this book be your compass. Let it guide you through the shadows, illuminate the hidden corners, and empower you to claim your rightful place in the world. For the introverted path to success is not just a choice for individuals, but a movement for change, a revolution in the definition of what it means to thrive. And you, my friend, are a vital part of that revolution.

Together, let us rewrite the narrative, not just for ourselves, but for generations of introverts to come. Let us show the world the power of quiet strength, the wisdom of introspection, and the beauty of success that blooms in the shadows. This is your story, your life, your introverted path to success. Take a deep breath, step into the unknown, and let your quiet light shine.

Chapter 1: Embracing Introversion

1.1 Understanding Your Strengths

In a world that roars with extroverted energy, where constant connection and social prowess reign supreme, it's easy for introverts to feel like muted instruments in a loud orchestra. Our quietude can be mistaken for apathy, our need for solitude for social ineptitude. But within the hushed castle of our introverted minds lie hidden strengths, potent tools waiting to be wielded for success on our own terms.

The Power of Deep Thinking

Forget the fleeting fireworks of quick wit and banter. We, the introverts, are the architects of slow-burning insights, the alchemists who transmute observations into profound understanding. Imagine a mind like a vast, subterranean cavern, where ideas echo and reverberate, each one meticulously examined and refined before rising to the surface. This is the introverted mind, a crucible where thoughts simmer and simmer, forging connections and nuances invisible to the hurried eye. While extroverts thrive on the immediacy of action and interaction, introverts possess a unique power – the power of deep thinking.

This inward steps isn't a retreat from reality; it's a strategic dive into its depths. Introverts have the inclination and capacity to delve into the complexities of a problem, to turn it over and over in their minds, scrutinizing its every facet. This introspective view allows them to unearth hidden patterns, anticipate potential pitfalls, and craft solutions that hold the weight of thorough consideration.

In the world of business, where decisions can make or break empires, this introverted strength shines brightly. Imagine a financial analyst, quietly dissecting market trends, unearthing correlations missed by the herd, and crafting a strategy that weathers the storm while others scramble for shelter. Or a scientist, patiently unraveling the mysteries of the universe, their focused contemplation leading to breakthroughs that rewrite textbooks.

Observation as Your Secret Weapon
While others bask in the limelight, we, the introverts, sit quietly at the periphery, absorbing the world with the keen eyes of a hawk. We notice the subtle shifts in body language, the flicker of doubt in a confident gaze, the unspoken emotions that betray outward smiles. While extroverts navigate the world through a kaleidoscope of external stimuli, introverts possess a keen eye for the subtle shifts and nuances that often go unnoticed. They are the silent observers, the watchful sentinels who absorb the world around them like a sponge, meticulously cataloging every detail. This introspective observation isn't mere idle curiosity; it's a powerful tool for understanding the intricacies of human behavior and the dynamics of the world around us.

Imagine a writer, weaving characters and narratives so real they leap off the page, their insights into human emotions gleaned from years of quiet observation. Or a politician, navigating the delicate balance of diplomacy, their understanding of social cues and unspoken tensions honed through attentive observation.

In a world where data reigns supreme, the introverted observer holds a unique advantage. They can analyze customer behavior, predict market trends, and anticipate social shifts with a precision that eludes others. Their quiet attentiveness allows them to grasp the unspoken language of body language, facial expressions, and subtle shifts in tone, making them invaluable assets in any field that requires a deep understanding of human behavior.

Creativity Unleashed

Society often paints introverts as dry and logical, devoid of the fire of artistic expression. Yet, within our quiet souls burn the embers of unbridled creativity. Unhampered by the need for constant external validation, we are free to explore the boundless landscapes of our imaginations. Introversion isn't a synonym for dullness; it's a breeding ground for creativity. While extroverts find inspiration in the buzz of social interaction, introverts draw their creative fuel from the quiet chambers of their minds. Unburdened by the constant need for external stimuli, they can delve into the depths of their imagination, crafting worlds unseen and stories unheard.

Imagine a musician, their introspective nature allowing them to tap into the deepest wells of emotion, weaving melodies that resonate with the soul. Or an artist, their solitude a canvas for their imagination, birthing masterpieces that challenge and inspire.

The introverted creative process is a tapestry woven from solitude, introspection, and focused attention. It's a slow burn, a gradual unfolding of ideas that have been nurtured in the fertile soil of the mind. This introspective approach allows introverts to create with a depth and authenticity that resonates with audiences on a profound level.

Understanding your strengths isn't just about self-discovery; it's about unleashing your potential to achieve remarkable things. The world needs your introverted superpower – your deep thinking, your keen observation, your creative spark. It needs your unique perspective, your ability to see beyond the surface and dive into the depths of complexity.

So, introverted achiever, cast aside the misconceptions and societal pressures that tell you to be louder, faster, bolder. Embrace your quiet power. Hone your deep thinking skills, refine your observation, and unleash your introspective creativity. This is your time, your moment to show the world the extraordinary power that lies within the introverted mind.

1.2 Debunking Introvert Myths

For centuries, introverts have been misunderstood, mislabeled, and even ostracized. Our quiet nature, preference for solitude, and introspective tendencies have been misconstrued as shyness, social awkwardness, or even a lack of character. But what if the truth is far more nuanced? What if introversion, instead of being a weakness, is a powerful set of strengths waiting to be unleashed?

Myth #1: Introverts are Shy

The introvert archetype often gets painted as a timid soul clinging to the shadows, terrified of social interaction. Yet, shyness and introversion are distinct entities. Shyness is characterized by a fear of social interaction and a reluctance to engage with others. Introverts, on the other hand, simply gain energy from solitude and require periods of quiet to recharge. While some introverts may also be shy, the vast majority are not. In fact, many introverts are skilled communicators, insightful observers, and deeply empathetic individuals who simply prefer smaller, more meaningful interactions.

Think of it this way: a flower basking in the sun thrives on its warmth, while a nocturnal creature draws energy from the moonlit night. Both are vital to the ecosystem, yet their needs and preferences differ. Similarly, introverts and extroverts are not opposites, but rather members of the same human spectrum, each with their own unique strengths and contributions.

So, the next time someone labels you as shy because you prefer a quiet corner to a crowded room, politely correct them. Explain that you're not shy, you're simply an introvert who needs time to recharge and process information in a different way. By educating others about the true nature of introversion, we chip away at the myth and pave the way for acceptance and understanding.

Myth #2: Introverts are Antisocial

Another damaging misconception is that introverts are antisocial loners who shun all human interaction. This couldn't be further from the truth. Introverts crave connection, just like everyone else. We build deep and meaningful relationships, often preferring small, intimate gatherings over large, boisterous crowds. We listen intently, offer thoughtful advice, and value genuine conversations over superficial small talk.

Imagine a sculptor meticulously carving a masterpiece. Each stroke is deliberate, focused, and precise. Introverts are like that sculptor, investing time and energy into cultivating meaningful connections, one at a time. We may not be the life of the party, but we are the confidantes, the deep thinkers, the loyal friends who offer unwavering support and understanding.

So, the next time someone asks why you prefer intimate dinners to loud parties, don't apologize. Explain that your social energy is precious and you choose to invest it in those who truly matter. Remind them that quality connections are more valuable than quantity, and that introverts, with their deliberate approach to relationships, are often the ones who build the most lasting bonds.

Myth #3: All Introverts are the Same

Perhaps the most damaging myth of all is the assumption that all introverts are a homogenous group with identical personalities and preferences. This is simply not true. Introversion is a spectrum, with individuals falling anywhere along the line from highly introverted to ambiverted (a blend of introversion and extroversion). Just as snowflakes are unique, so too are introverts.

Think of it like a vast, diverse forest. Some trees stand tall and proud in open meadows, basking in the sunlight. Others thrive in the sheltered shade of the undergrowth, quietly absorbing the dappled light. Both contribute to the beauty and richness of the forest, even though their appearances and preferences differ. Similarly, introverts exhibit a wide range of personalities, interests, and talents. We are artists, scientists, entrepreneurs, leaders, and everything in between.

So, the next time someone tries to define you based on a single stereotype, remember your individuality. Embrace the unique qualities that make you who you are, whether it's your analytical mind, your creative spirit, or your unwavering loyalty. Celebrate the diversity of introverted personalities and remind the world that introverts are not a monolith, but a vibrant framework of individuals enriching the world in countless ways.

Debunking these myths is not just about clearing the air; it's about reclaiming your power and identity. By understanding and embracing your introverted nature, you tap into a reservoir of strengths you may not have even realized you possessed.

1.3 Introverted Success Metrics

The world celebrates a singular brand of success. Loud victors, extroverted leaders, and masters of the social game paint the picture of achievement in bold, vibrant colors. But what if that canvas doesn't hold space for you, the quiet observer, the deep thinker, the introverted architect of your own dreams? What if success, for you, whispers in a different language, measured not in decibels but in depth, not in accolades but in fulfillment?

Reclaiming Success for Your Introverted Soul

Society's definition of success is a cacophony of external validations: climbing the corporate ladder, amassing wealth, accumulating accolades. While these achievements can certainly bring satisfaction, for introverts, they often come at the cost of draining our energy reserves and compromising our core needs for solitude and reflection. We may find ourselves excelling in these arenas, yet harboring a nagging sense of emptiness, like trophies gathering dust in a dimly lit corner of our souls.

Forget the blaring headlines, the viral dances, and the podiums bathed in applause. These may be the currency of the extroverted world, but they hold little value in the introverted realm. Success, for you, lies not in external validation, but in the quiet satisfaction of a job well done, the deep resonance with your own values, and the lasting impact you create in ways that resonate with your introverted nature.

Imagine success not as a trophy on the mantelpiece, but as a meticulously crafted mosaic, each piece carefully chosen, reflecting your values, passions, and strengths. It's the joy of mastering a skill you've always admired, the thrill of solving a complex problem with elegant simplicity, the quiet satisfaction of creating something that resonates deeply with your own soul.

The Mastery Mindset

For us, achievement takes on a different hue. It's not about reaching the highest rung of the ladder, but about climbing with meticulous focus, savoring the intricacies of each step, honing our skills to a razor's edge. We are the artisans of expertise, the silent sculptors of knowledge, finding pleasure in the process of refining our craft, not just the final product.

While the extroverted world thrives on external validation, introverts find their fuel in the fire of internal mastery. We are the architects of our own excellence, meticulously honing our skills, refining our knowledge, and pushing the boundaries of our own understanding. This isn't about blind ambition; it's about a quiet, relentless pursuit of personal growth, a dedication to becoming the best version of ourselves, not for the applause of others, but for the profound satisfaction of knowing we have reached our full potential.

Picture a sculptor, alone in their studio, chipping away at a block of stone, not for the gallery opening, but for the love of the craft, the thrill of revealing the form hidden within. This is the mastery mindset, an introverted superpower that allows us to excel in fields where deep thought, meticulous execution, and unwavering focus are the keys to success.

Creating a Ripple Effect That Aligns with Your Values

Our impact, too, resonates on a different frequency. While extroverts tend to broadcast their contributions, introverts often leave their mark through subtle shifts, quiet interventions, and long-lasting ripples that spread in the wake of their thoughtful actions.

For many introverts, the true measure of success isn't individual achievement, but the positive impact it creates on the world around them. We are driven by a sense of purpose, a desire to leave the world a little better than we found it. But our contributions, like the roots of a mighty oak, often run deep and silent, shaping the landscape in subtle yet profound ways.

Imagine a writer, crafting stories in the quiet hours, not for the bestseller lists, but for the power they hold to touch hearts, spark conversations, and inspire change. Or a scientist, diligently analyzing data, not for the accolades, but for the potential to unlock a breakthrough that benefits humanity. These are the ripples of introverted impact, quietly changing the world without the need for a megaphone.

So, how do you, the introverted navigator, chart your course to success? The first step is introspection. Look inward, identify your core values, the things that truly matter to you. Is it creativity, knowledge, connection, or perhaps a sense of purpose and service? These are your guiding stars, the compass that will lead you through the noisy extroverted world and towards the quiet fulfillment that awaits.

Once you have identified your values, let them be the filters through which you evaluate every opportunity, every decision. Is this career path aligned with your introverted strengths? Does this project resonate with your desire for deep connection or quiet contemplation? Are these relationships nurturing your need for genuine interaction and meaningful exchange?

Success for an introvert is not a one-size-fits-all suit. It's a bespoke garment, tailored to your unique strengths, values, and preferences. Embrace the quiet power of your introversion, redefine success on your own terms, and steps on a path of personal mastery that leaves an impact far beyond the fleeting applause of the extroverted world.

Chapter 2: Navigating the Introverted Landscape

2.1 Psychological Foundations of Introversion

Imagine yourself standing at the edge of a vast, verdant forest. Sunlight filters through the canopy, dappling the ground with a mosaic of light and shadow. The air hums with the symphony of unseen life, a gentle counterpoint to the rustle of leaves beneath your feet. This, in many ways, is the introverted landscape. A world where inner experience blooms alongside external stimuli, where reflection reigns alongside action, and where solitude finds its sweet solace.

But why do we stand at the edge, peering into this introspective realm? Because understanding the psychological foundations of introversion is the first step in navigating its terrain, in learning to not just survive, but thrive within its unique ecosystem.

Exploring the Roots of Introversion

The question of why some individuals are drawn to the introverted path has long captivated psychologists. While the exact cause remains a fascinating tapestry woven from genetics, environment, and even brain chemistry, several prominent theories offer intriguing glimpses.

1. The Arousal Model: Proposed by Hans Eysenck, this theory suggests that introverts have a heightened sensitivity to external stimulation. Their brains, already buzzing with internal activity, become easily overwhelmed by the

barrage of sights, sounds, and sensations that fill the world around them. Introverts, therefore, seek solitude or quieter environments to restore their internal equilibrium.

2. The Reward System Theory: This theory, championed by Elaine Aron, proposes that introverts experience intrinsic rewards differently. While extroverts find their dopamine fountain activated by external stimuli like social interaction, introverts derive greater pleasure from internal activities like introspection, deep thinking, and creative pursuits. This difference in reward pathways explains why introverts naturally gravitate towards activities that nourish their inner world.

3. The Evolutionary Model: Some researchers suggest that introversion may have offered an evolutionary advantage in our hunter-gatherer past. While extroverts excelled at social coordination and group hunting, introverts, with their keen observation skills and focus on internal processing, may have been adept at solitary tasks like trapping and scouting. This diversity of skills ensured the survival of the tribe, even as individual preferences led to different paths.

Understanding the Spectrum of Introverted Traits
Introversion is not a binary switch. It exists on a beautiful continuum, a spectrum where individual shades and nuances play out. Some introverts find joy in small social gatherings, while others prefer complete solitude. Some thrive in leadership roles, wielding their quiet strength and strategic thinking, while others find comfort in supporting

roles, contributing through their thoughtful analysis and meticulous execution.

Here are some key dimensions within the introverted landscape

- Social Energy Levels: Some introverts have high social energy but expend it quickly, needing to recharge in solitude. Others have naturally low social energy and prefer smaller doses of interaction.

- Social Comfort Zones: Some introverts excel in one-on-one conversations, while others find even close interactions draining. Some enjoy online communication, while others prefer face-to-face interactions.

- Expression of Thought: Some introverts are natural communicators, articulating their ideas with clarity and precision. Others prefer to process internally, expressing their thoughts through writing, art, or even silence.

- Need for Stimulation: Some introverts crave stimulation, seeking out intellectual challenges and creative outlets. Others prefer a calmer pace, finding satisfaction in quiet contemplation and simple pleasures.

This spectrum is not about right or wrong, strong or weak. It is about recognizing and embracing the unique blend of traits that define your own introverted personality.

Navigating Life Based on Personal Preferences

Understanding your personal preferences within the introverted landscape empowers you to navigate life with intentionality. Here are some key strategies:

- Honor your need for solitude: Schedule time for yourself, whether it's a daily meditation session, a weekend retreat in nature, or simply an evening spent curled up with a good book.

- Choose your social interactions wisely: Prioritize quality over quantity, surrounding yourself with people who respect your introverted nature and engage in meaningful conversations.

- Communicate your needs: Don't shy away from explaining your preferences. Let people know you may need to recharge after social gatherings or that you prefer smaller, more intimate settings.

- Find your outlets: Explore activities that nourish your inner world, whether it's creative pursuits, intellectual challenges, or simply spending time in introspective reflection.

- Embrace your strengths: Introverts possess valuable qualities like focus, depth of thought, and a strong sense of self-awareness. These strengths can be leveraged in various fields, from leadership roles to creative endeavors to analytical positions.

Delving into the psychological foundations of introversion is more than just intellectual exercise. It's a fertile ground for self-acceptance and empowerment. By understanding the why behind our tendencies, we can cultivate a sense of agency and confidence. We can begin to see our introversion not as a weakness, but as a unique set of strengths, a different lens through which we experience the world and contribute to it.

2.2 Types of Introverts

The term "introvert" paints a broad stroke, encompassing a multitude of personalities and experiences. While introversion shares a common thread of prioritizing inner stimulation and needing time alone to recharge, it blossoms into a diverse tapestry within each individual. Delving into the spectrum of introverted personalities is not just an intellectual exercise; it's a story of self-discovery, a key to unlocking your unique potential for success.

1. The Social Introvert

For the social introvert, the world is a bustling marketplace where small talk feels like a foreign language. Crowds are not energizing, but draining, and the constant hum of social interaction can feel like white noise. Yet, to label them as "anti-social" is to miss the mark entirely. Social introverts crave meaningful connections, preferring depth over breadth, quality over quantity. Think of them as connoisseurs of conversation, savoring genuine exchanges over fleeting acquaintances.

Their strength lies in their laser focus on building meaningful relationships. They listen intently, absorb information like sponges, and offer thoughtful responses that resonate. In a world obsessed with superficiality, the social introvert's authenticity is a refreshing counterpoint. They are the confidantes, the trusted advisors, the friends who see you, not just the persona you project.

Socializing for them is a focused, purposeful act, not a marathon of small talk. While large crowds drain them, one-on-one connections fill their energy reserves, leaving them brimming with ideas and observations to share. For social introverts, success lies in recognizing their social sweet spot, crafting environments that nurture meaningful interactions, and mastering the art of graceful exits when the energy bank dips.

Their challenge, however, lies in finding their own rhythm in the social interaction. Mastering the art of selective engagement is key. Learning to politely decline invitations that drain their energy while prioritizing those that offer genuine connection is crucial. Remember, social introverts, your presence, even in smaller doses, can have a profound impact. Choose your interactions wisely, and let your genuine nature shine through.

2. The Analytical Introvert

Thinking introverts are the architects of inner worlds, where ideas moves and theories take shape. Imagine a meticulous builder, piecing together intricate structures of thought, lost in the quiet hum of their own minds. They thrive on deep contemplation, relishing the intricate puzzles of the world and dissecting them with laser focus.

For the analytical introvert, the world is a puzzle waiting to be solved. Their minds are intricate labyrinths, constantly churning with ideas, analyzing, dissecting, and reconstructing information. They are the architects of thought, meticulously constructing frameworks of knowledge, testing hypotheses, and seeking the hidden logic behind everything.

Their strength lies in their deep well of contemplation. They can dissect complex problems with laser-like precision, identify hidden patterns, and formulate innovative solutions. In a world of impulsive decisions and superficial trends, the analytical introvert's thoughtful approach is a valuable asset. They are the strategists, the problem solvers, the ones who see the bigger picture before the brushstrokes are even applied. They excel at strategic planning, meticulous analysis, and problem-solving with elegant solutions that often surprise with their originality. For analytical introverts, success lies in carving out dedicated spaces for uninterrupted thinking, mastering the art of concise communication to share their insights, and finding like-minded collaborators who appreciate the depth and precision of their thought. Social interaction, while not unwelcome, can feel like a detour from their internal symphony. Yet, their introspective nature is a treasure trove of wisdom and insight.

However, their challenge lies in translating their internal brilliance into external action. Their meticulous nature can lead to procrastination, waiting for the perfect moment to unveil their carefully crafted solutions. Remember, analytical introverts, the world needs your insights. Don't let the fear of imperfection paralyze your progress. Share your ideas, even in their nascent form, and embrace the power of collaboration to refine and implement your genius.

3. The Spectrum of Introversion

The landscape of introversion is not a binary of social and analytical. The introverted landscape is not limited to these two prominent peaks. Anxious introverts, for example, may navigate social situations with a touch of trepidation, their internal compass ever vigilant for potential pitfalls. They crave connection but can feel overwhelmed by the cacophony of external stimuli. Restrained introverts, on the other hand, are the masters of self-control, carefully weighing their actions and words before venturing out. They value thoughtfulness over impulsivity and may appear reserved at first glance, yet their quiet observations hold a depth that shines through with time.

Some introverts may find solace in solitude, while others thrive in small, intimate groups. Some may be energized by creative pursuits, while others find solace in the quiet hum of routine. The key is to identify the threads that make up your unique tapestry and embrace their unique blend.

There are the creative introverts, their minds brimming with artistic expression, their souls whispering stories in melodies and brushstrokes. There are the introspective introverts, their inner world a playground for philosophical musing and self-discovery. There are even the pragmatic introverts, their focus on efficiency and organization making them masters of logistics and meticulous planning.

No matter where you fall on the spectrum, remember this: your introversion is not a weakness to overcome, but a strength to cultivate. It is the lens through which you perceive the world, the source of your unique insights, and the foundation upon which you build your success.

Embracing the spectrum of introverted personalities allows us to build communities of understanding and support. Social introverts can learn from the analytical minds to articulate their insights, while analytical introverts can benefit from the social butterfly's ease of connection. Anxious introverts can find solace in the quiet confidence of restrained introverts, and vice versa. By recognizing the strengths and challenges inherent in each type, we can create a framework of introverted success that is not only diverse, but also harmoniously woven together.

Remember, your introverted nature is not a limitation, but a unique lens through which you experience the world. By understanding your own type, appreciating the spectrum, and embracing your introverted strengths, you can forge a path to success that is authentic, fulfilling, and uniquely yours.

2.3 Navigating Social Energy

Imagine your social energy as a vibrant battery powering your interactions with the world. Like any resource, it depletes through use, and for introverts, the recharge cycle can be longer and more crucial. Mastering the art of managing this energy is the cornerstone of thriving in a world often clamoring for our extroverted counterparts.

Managing and Replenishing Energy Levels

For introverts, social interactions can be both enriching and draining. The key lies in understanding one's energy threshold and implementing strategies to manage and replenish it. It begins with self-awareness — recognizing when social interactions are invigorating and when they become exhausting.

Understanding the Drain:

Firstly, recognizing the unique impact of social interaction on introverts is essential. Every conversation, every gathering, chips away at your social energy reserve, unlike extroverts who often find these interactions energizing. This isn't a defect; it's simply a different wiring, akin to needing different amounts of sleep. Don't mistake social exhaustion for shyness or disinterest; it's simply your internal gauge signaling "recharge required."

Mapping Your Limits:

Just as we wouldn't run our phones on 5% battery, ignoring our social energy depletion leads to burnout. Become hyper-aware of your individual triggers. Is it small talk draining your tank? Large crowds? Extended work meetings? Pinpointing these energy vampires equips you to avoid or mitigate their impact. Listen to your body – that subtle fatigue, the tightening in your chest, the craving for solitude – these are your body's wisdom cries, not flaws to dismiss.

The Recharge Revolution:

Now, the art of replenishment. Remember, introverts require intentional charging stations, not fleeting top-ups. Prioritize solitude as a sanctuary, not a luxury. Schedule "alone time" like any crucial appointment. Whether it's a solo morning coffee, a rejuvenating afternoon nap, or an evening lost in a captivating book, build these refuges into your daily routine. Disconnect from the digital world; let your phone become a tool, not a leash. Savor silence, immerse yourself in nature, indulge in activities that nourish your inner world. These are not escapes; they are vital investments in your social stamina.

Setting Powerful Boundaries

Setting boundaries is an integral aspect of preserving social energy. Introverts should feel empowered to establish limits on the duration and frequency of social engagements. Communicating these boundaries openly and assertively is crucial. This involves expressing the need for downtime without apology, allowing for a harmonious balance between social obligations and personal recharge.

Master the art of declining invitations gracefully, without guilt or elaborate justifications. "Thank you, but I have a full plate tomorrow" or "I need some quiet time after work today" are perfectly valid responses. Don't let social obligations become energy debt collectors. Conversely, learn to curate your "yeses." Prioritize interactions that resonate with your interests and fuel your spirit. Seek out fellow introverts or individuals who respect your need for personal space. Quality over quantity becomes your mantra.

Navigating the Social Maze
Social interactions needn't be exhausting battlegrounds. Introverts often possess keen observation skills and thoughtful conversational depths, strengths that can shine in the right settings. Here are some strategies to thrive:

- Embrace one-on-one interactions: Small, focused conversations allow you to truly connect and avoid the overwhelming stimuli of large groups.

- Become a master of "small talk escape routes": Have a "phone call" excuse ready, or politely excuse yourself to refill your drink – anything to regain your equilibrium.

- Contribute in your own way: Don't force yourself to be the life of the party. Offer thoughtful comments, contribute insightful questions, or lend a supportive ear. Your quiet presence can be just as valuable.

- Harness the power of technology: Online communities, virtual gatherings, and asynchronous communication tools allow you to connect on your own terms.

Remember, thriving as an introvert isn't about shunning the world; it's about navigating it on your own terms. By understanding your energy rhythms, setting boundaries, and strategically recharging, you can confidently navigate the social landscape without sacrificing your precious peace or introverted essence. Embrace your need for solitude, honor your energy limits, and discover the joy of connecting authentically within the social sphere. The world needs your unique perspective, introverted friend, and it can be experienced beautifully, in your own way, one replenished social interaction at a time.

Chapter 3: Success Strategies in an Extroverted World

3.1 Effective Communication for Introverts

For many introverts, communication in an extroverted world feels like traversing a jungle gym sculpted by extroverts, for extroverts. Loud chatter echoes on every rung, boisterous energy swings from bar to bar, and the expectation to constantly perform leaps and bounds can seem utterly exhausting. Yet, communication lies at the heart of navigating any success domain, be it building fulfilling careers, fostering meaningful relationships, or advocating for your ideas. For introverts, the key lies not in mimicking the extroverted symphony, but in mastering your own instrument, playing your unique melody with both clarity and confidence.

Developing Assertiveness

Introverts often fall prey to the misconception that assertiveness translates to loudness, to dominating conversations with force and fanfare. It's a misinterpretation that leaves us shrinking back, our valuable thoughts and ideas trapped within. True assertiveness, however, is about claiming your right to be heard, to express your needs and opinions with clarity and conviction, regardless of the decibel level. It's about speaking your truth without apology, and standing firm in your beliefs without aggression.

The Tools of Assertion:

- Body language: Stand tall, maintain eye contact, and use confident gestures. Nonverbal cues can speak volumes before you even utter a word.

- Clear and concise communication: Avoid rambling or apologizing for your presence. State your points directly and succinctly, leaving no room for misinterpretation.

- Active listening: Truly hear what others are saying before formulating your response. This demonstrates respect and builds trust, making your own voice even more impactful when raised.

- Setting boundaries: Learn to say "no" gracefully but firmly when overwhelmed or asked to do something outside your comfort zone. Your time and energy are valuable, and protecting them is key to assertive communication.

Practice Makes Perfect:

Role-playing scenarios with trusted friends or family can help you hone your assertiveness muscles in a safe environment. Start with simple situations like expressing a preference for lunch or disagreeing with a minor point, then gradually progress to more complex scenarios like asking for a raise or handling a heated negotiation. Remember, assertiveness is a skill that develops with practice, and every "no" uttered with conviction paves the way for your voice to be heard with respect.

Strategies for Confident Self-Expression

While introverts often possess deep thoughts and insightful observations, sharing them in an extroverted world can feel daunting. We may worry about rambling, losing our train of thought under the spotlight, or simply not being interesting enough to hold the attention of an audience. Yet, within our introverted reserves lies a wealth of knowledge and unique perspectives waiting to be unleashed. Here are some strategies to confidently express yourself, whether in one-on-one conversations or larger gatherings:

- Preparation is key: Whether it's a casual chat or a formal presentation, take time to gather your thoughts beforehand. Jot down key points, anticipate potential questions, and rehearse your delivery if necessary. Confidence grows with preparation, allowing you to face any conversation with composure.

- Embrace the power of silence: Don't feel pressured to fill every pause. Introverts often benefit from strategic silence, giving them time to process information and formulate thoughtful responses. Let your pauses add weight to your words, not create awkwardness.

- Leverage your strengths: Introverts tend to be excellent listeners, observant, and thoughtful communicators. Use these strengths to your advantage. Ask insightful questions, connect with others on a deeper level, and share your unique perspective on the world. People are drawn to genuine conversations, not extroverted noise.

- Find your comfort zone: Not all communication channels are created equal. Embrace written communication where you can craft your thoughts with precision, or utilize technology like email or messaging platforms to express yourself at your own pace. Stepping outside your comfort zone occasionally is good for growth, but knowing your safe havens helps you recharge and navigate social situations with confidence.

The Power of Storytelling:

Sharing personal anecdotes and experiences can be a powerful tool for engaging both introverts and extroverts. Choose stories that highlight your strengths, values, or unique perspective. Weaving narrative threads into your communication adds an element of human connection, making your introverted voice resonate even more deeply. Remember, authenticity is key. Don't force yourself into an extroverted mold simply to entertain. Share your stories with sincerity and passion, and let your natural introverted style add a touch of depth and nuance to the conversation.

Navigating Common Workplace Communication Challenges

The workplace, with its constant meetings, networking events, and open-plan offices, can feel like the Mount Everest of social interaction for introverts. But just like scaling a mountain, reaching the summit requires the right tools and strategies. Here's how to tackle those common workplace communication challenges with grace and efficiency:

Meetings:

- Prepare beforehand: Review agendas, anticipate key points, and formulate questions you might want to ask. This prevents feeling lost or overwhelmed during the discussion.

- Contribute strategically: Don't wait for the perfect moment to chime in. If you have a valuable point, voice it confidently, even if it means interrupting briefly. Introverts often possess unique perspectives that can enrich discussions.

- Embrace asynchronous communication: Utilize email, project management tools, or internal messaging platforms to share your ideas or feedback. This allows you to communicate effectively on your own terms, without the pressure of real-time interactions.

Feedback:

- Seek meaningful feedback: Don't shy away from seeking constructive criticism from trusted colleagues or mentors. This can help you identify areas for improvement and refine your skills.

- Listen actively and process thoughtfully: Don't react defensively to feedback. Take time to understand the message, ask clarifying questions if needed, and then formulate a thoughtful response. Remember, feedback is an opportunity for growth, not a personal attack.

- Communicate your needs: If you find feedback sessions overwhelming, advocate for settings that cater to your introverted preferences. One-on-one meetings, written feedback reports, or asynchronous conversations can create a more comfortable and productive environment.

Building Relationships:

- Focus on quality over quantity: Instead of aiming for a wide circle of acquaintances, invest in building deep and meaningful connections with a few like-minded colleagues. Introverts naturally thrive in smaller, more intimate settings.

- Leverage your strengths: Utilize your active listening skills to build rapport, your thoughtful observations to offer insightful advice, and your written communication skills to express your appreciation or support.

- Embrace your networking style: Don't force yourself into crowded mixers or large social gatherings. Seek out networking opportunities that cater to introverts, such as one-on-one coffee meetings, industry conferences with focused sessions, or online communities with shared interests. Remember, networking is about building genuine connections, not winning a popularity contest.

Don't feel pressured to conform to an extroverted ideal. By honing your assertiveness, confidently expressing yourself, and navigating workplace challenges with your unique strengths, you can carve your own path to success, leaving an indelible mark on the world, one well-placed, thoughtful step at a time. The jungle gym of an extroverted world may seem daunting, but with the right tools and strategies, you can not only survive but thrive, proving that introverts have just as much, if not more, to offer than their extroverted counterparts.

3.2 Thriving in Extroverted Workplaces

The modern office. Open-plan landscapes filled with animated chatter, conference rooms buzzing with brainstorming sessions, and corridors perpetually throbbing with the pulse of self-promotion. For an introvert, it can feel like entering a whirlwind, leaving you drained and disoriented. But hold your retreat, dear introvert! Success in extroverted workplaces doesn't require morphing into an extrovert clone. It's about harnessing your strengths, wielding your unique skills, and navigating the social currents with quiet confidence.

Strategies for Success in Office Landscapes Built for Extroverts

1. Embrace the power of "quiet focus": While the office hums with activity, you have the advantage of carving out your own oasis of calm. Use noise-canceling headphones, seek out quiet corners, or schedule focused work time early in the morning or late in the evening. Remember, introverts excel at deep thinking and meticulous execution, which thrives in environments free from constant distractions.

2. Master the art of strategic interaction: Don't shy away from social interactions altogether. Engage in focused, meaningful conversations with colleagues who share your interests or whom you can learn from. Participate in relevant meetings, offering concise and insightful contributions when the time is right. Remember, quality trumps quantity. A well-placed, thoughtful comment can have far more impact than a constant stream of chatter.

3. Become a champion of asynchronous communication: Utilize email, project management tools, and internal messaging platforms to your advantage. This allows you to express your ideas clearly and concisely on your own terms, avoiding the pressure of on-the-spot thinking during meetings or spontaneous office interactions.

4. Leverage your strengths as a team player: Introverts often possess exceptional listening skills, keen observation abilities, and a talent for analyzing data and providing thoughtful solutions. Contribute these strengths to team projects, offering valuable insights and collaborating effectively in smaller, focused groups. Remember, your introverted nature is not a handicap but a valuable asset to any team.

5. Create boundaries to protect your energy: Set clear limits on your social interactions, particularly during periods of intense work or after particularly draining activities. Learn to politely decline invitations or excuse yourself from conversations when feeling overwhelmed. Don't apologize for needing your introverted recharge time – it's essential for your well-being and productivity.

Navigating Office Politics with Authenticity

1. Sharpen your emotional intelligence: Understanding the unspoken dynamics of office politics is crucial for any professional, regardless of personality type. Observe how relationships unfold, identify key players, and pay attention to unspoken cues. This awareness will help you navigate the social landscape with grace and avoid potential pitfalls.

2. Seek strategic alliances: Find mentors, sponsors, or allies who appreciate your introverted strengths and can advocate for you in situations where your voice might not be heard as readily. These connections can provide valuable guidance and open doors to new opportunities.

3. Focus on building trust and respect: While self-promotion might be the extrovert's forte, introverts can earn recognition through consistent excellence, reliable execution, and unwavering integrity. Deliver on your promises, exceed expectations, and be known for your quiet competence. People will take notice, and your reputation will speak volumes, even without the fanfare.

4. Be prepared to advocate for yourself, confidently but modestly: When opportunities arise, step forward and present your ideas with clarity and conviction. Highlight your successes and contributions, but do so with humility and focus on the value you bring to the table. Remember, your introverted nature doesn't diminish your achievements or expertise – it simply necessitates a different approach to self-promotion.

5. Don't engage in gossip or negativity: Stay above the fray of office politics by avoiding drama and gossip. Focus on

your own work, maintain positive relationships with colleagues, and cultivate an atmosphere of trust and respect. This approach will ensure you are seen as a reliable and stable force in the often-turbulent waters of office politics.

Networking Tips for Introverts in Professional Settings

1. Seek out like-minded individuals: Attend industry events or conferences focused on specific topics that interest you. This allows you to connect with fellow introverts who share your passion and interests, building meaningful relationships without the overwhelm of large, boisterous gatherings.

2. Utilize online communities: Professional networking platforms and online forums offer introverts a comfortable space to connect with colleagues and industry professionals. Participate in discussions, share your expertise, and build your network gradually, at your own pace.

3. Embrace one-on-one interactions: Instead of large networking events, focus on building strong connections with colleagues and industry professionals through individual meetings or coffee dates. This allows you to engage in focused conversations, get to know someone on a deeper level, and build genuine relationships that can lead to valuable opportunities.

4. Turn your strengths into networking tools: Your introverted nature fosters the ability to listen intently, ask insightful questions, and offer thoughtful observations. Leverage these skills to build genuine connections with individuals. Remember, networking is about quality, not quantity. A single meaningful conversation can be more valuable than a room full of fleeting encounters.

5. Become known as the "thoughtful communicator": Craft concise and impactful emails, prepare presentations that deliver clear insights, and contribute to online forums with well-researched comments. Demonstrating your expertise through written and online communication helps your introverted voice resonate without the pressure of face-to-face interactions.

6. Embrace technology as your networking ally: Utilize video conferencing tools to participate in meetings or connect with colleagues remotely. This allows you to contribute on your own terms, avoiding the draining energy of crowded conference rooms or noisy open offices.

The steps is just as important as the destination. Don't be discouraged if success doesn't come overnight. Building a successful career in an extroverted world takes time, patience, and unwavering self-belief. Focus on progress, not perfection. Believe in your ability to succeed on your own terms. Don't compare yourself to the extroverted ideal; instead, focus on honing your own unique strengths. Celebrate your victories, big and small, and learn from your setbacks. With perseverance and a commitment to authenticity, you can carve your own path to success in even the most extroverted of workplaces.

3.3 Introvert in Leadership

The world of leadership often paints a picture of charismatic figures, commanding attention with booming voices and extroverted energy. But what if a different kind of leader exists, one who navigates the terrain of success with quiet confidence and thoughtful vision? This is the realm of the introverted leader, where quiet strength holds the reins, and introspective wisdom guides the way.

Embracing Introverted Leadership Styles

1. The Power of the Quiet Leader: Introverts often possess inherent strengths that translate into powerful leadership qualities. Deep listening skills allow them to truly hear and understand their team members' needs and concerns. Their ability to focus and analyze information leads to well-informed decisions and meticulous planning. And their thoughtful, introspective approach fosters a culture of reflection and strategic thinking within the team. Introverts excel at deep thinking and meticulous planning. Leverage this strength to analyze situations, anticipate challenges, and craft well-considered strategies. Your ability to see the bigger picture and formulate thoughtful solutions will be invaluable in guiding your team through complex scenarios.

2. Leading by Example: Forget the loud pronouncements and grand gestures. Introverted leaders inspire by leading by example. Their consistent work ethic, unwavering dedication, and commitment to excellence set a clear standard for their team. They demonstrate the power of

quiet confidence, proving that strong leadership doesn't require constant self-promotion or a booming voice.

3. Leveraging the Power of Communication: Introverts may not crave the spotlight, but effective communication is still crucial for any leader. Hone your written communication skills, utilizing emails, reports, and project management tools to articulate your vision and clearly communicate expectations. In meetings, prepare concise and impactful presentations, focusing on the substance of your message rather than the theatrics. Remember, your thoughtful words can have a profound impact, even if delivered in a measured tone.

Balancing Authority with Introverted Tendencies

1. Finding Your Comfort Zone: Leading doesn't require constant social interaction. Delegate tasks effectively, schedule time for focused work, and create a leadership style that allows you to recharge and maintain your introverted energy. Remember, a well-rested and energized leader is a more effective leader.

2. Building Strong Subordinate Relationships: While you may not crave constant small talk, invest in building strong relationships with your team members. Schedule one-on-one meetings, actively listen to their concerns, and provide constructive feedback. Foster an environment of open communication and mutual respect, where your quiet leadership style is seen not as a weakness, but as a strength that allows for thoughtful decisions and personalized support.

3. Delegation and Empowerment: Don't try to control everything. Recognize your team members' strengths and delegate tasks accordingly. Empower them to take ownership, make decisions, and contribute their unique talents to the team's success. This not only lightens your load but also fosters a sense of trust and engagement within the team.

Navigating Team Dynamics as an Introverted Leader

1. Building a Cohesive Team: Introverted leaders often foster a collaborative environment where everyone's voice is heard and valued. Encourage open communication, brainstorm ideas together, and create a safe space for team members to share their thoughts and concerns. Remember, a diverse team is a strong team, and your introverted leadership style can create an environment where everyone feels comfortable contributing and reaching their full potential.

2. Dealing with Conflict: Conflict is inevitable in any team, and as a leader, it's your responsibility to navigate it effectively. Use your natural listening skills to understand different perspectives, focus on finding solutions rather than assigning blame, and encourage open and honest communication to resolve issues constructively. Remember, your calm demeanor and thoughtful approach can be invaluable in resolving conflict and maintaining a positive team dynamic. Be open to feedback from your team and colleagues, especially regarding your

communication style and leadership approach. Actively listen to their concerns, identify what you need to adjust and apply that as your strength.

3. Leading by Inspiration: Great leaders don't just tell, they inspire. Use your introspective nature to connect with your team on a deeper level. Share your vision, your passion for the project, and the values that drive you. When your team sees the genuine passion and commitment behind your quiet leadership, they will be naturally drawn to follow your lead.

Introverted leadership is not about mimicking an extroverted ideal. It's about embracing your unique strengths, leveraging your natural tendencies, and building a leadership style that allows you to thrive. By following these strategies, you can silence the doubts, claim your rightful place as a leader, and pave the way for a successful and fulfilling career, all while remaining true to your introverted nature.

Chapter 4: Crafting Your Introverted Success Path

4.1 Choosing Introvert-Friendly Careers

The career landscape often feels like a boisterous market square, buzzing with extroverted energy and demanding constant self-promotion. For introverts, the pressure to conform to this dynamic can be suffocating, leading to unfulfilled potential and a sense of dissonance. But the truth is, your introverted nature isn't a career handicap; it's a unique set of strengths waiting to be unlocked in the right environment.

Identifying Introvert-Friendly Work Environments

- Seek autonomy and independence: Introverts thrive in environments that offer freedom and structure. Look for careers that allow you to work independently, set your own pace, and manage your time effectively. Remote work opportunities, freelance gigs, and positions with minimal micromanagement can be ideal settings for introverted professionals.

- Embrace deep thought and focused work: Introverts excel at analyzing data, solving problems, and meticulously executing tasks. Seek out roles that value these deep-thinking and dedicated qualities. Research, data analysis, writing, programming, and analytical roles in various fields can provide the intellectual stimulation and focused work environment introverts crave. Identify industries and roles that prioritize in-depth analysis, independent research, and meticulous execution. Data analysis, research, writing, and design professions often offer introverts the opportunity to excel in environments that cater to their deep thinking and focused attention.

- Value thoughtful communication and collaboration: While loud meetings and constant socializing might drain introverts, meaningful conversations and focused collaboration hold immense value. Look for teams and companies that foster a culture of respect and open communication, where ideas are valued over volume, and collaboration happens strategically rather than constantly.

- Prioritize introverted recharge time: Maintaining your energy is crucial for success. Seek work environments that respect your need for solitude and recharge time. Flexible schedules, generous PTO policies, and the ability to work remotely can allow you to schedule breaks and maintain your introverted well-being without compromising productivity. Consider opportunities that allow you to work from the comfort of your own space, reducing the need for constant social interaction and allowing you to recharge during the workday. Remember, location isn't everything – ensure the work itself aligns with your strengths and interests.

Selecting Roles that Leverage Introverted Qualities
- Leverage your analytical prowess: Introverts naturally possess keen observation skills and excel at analyzing data. Consider careers in research, data analysis, financial planning, actuarial science, or other fields where your

ability to process information and identify patterns can be a valuable asset.

- Channel your strategic thinking: Your introspective nature allows you to consider multiple perspectives and develop well-thought-out plans. Embrace roles in strategic planning, project management, policy analysis, or consulting, where your strategic thinking and attention to detail will be appreciated.

- Harness your written communication skills: Introverts often excel at expressing themselves clearly and concisely in writing. Explore careers in technical writing, copywriting, content marketing, editing, or grant writing, where your written communication skills can shine.

- Embrace your creativity in solitude: Many introverts possess untapped creative potential that flourishes in quiet environments. Explore careers in writing, graphic design, photography, web development, or other creative fields where you can channel your creative energy at your own pace and produce impactful work.

- Utilize your listening and observation skills: Introverts are masters of attentive listening and keen observation. Consider careers in social work, counseling, psychology, customer service (focusing on written communication), or teaching, where your ability to understand people and their needs can be a transformative power.

Advocating for Flexibility and Autonomy in Career Choices

- Negotiate for introverted-friendly work arrangements: Don't shy away from discussing your introverted needs during job interviews or performance reviews. Advocate for flexible work schedules, remote work options, and quiet workspaces. Many companies are increasingly adapting to accommodate diverse work styles, and a genuine conversation can open doors to a more fulfilling work experience.

- Build your own path: Don't feel confined to traditional career structures. Consider freelancing, consulting, or entrepreneurship, where you can design your own work environment and leverage your introverted strengths on your own terms. Remember, success doesn't have to fit a mold; it can be found in crafting a path that aligns with your unique needs and preferences.

- Embrace the power of networking: While socializing in large groups might drain you, strategic networking can be invaluable for introverts. Build connections with like-minded professionals through online communities, industry events focused on specific topics, or one-on-one coffee meetings. This allows you to connect with potential employers or collaborators without the overwhelm of large, extroverted gatherings.

Choosing the right career path is not one step success. Explore, experiment, and be unafraid to advocate for your introverted needs. The world needs the unique perspective, analytical prowess, and thoughtful solutions that introverts bring to the table. By identifying the right environment and leveraging your strengths, you can craft a career that not only fuels your success but also allows you to flourish as your authentic introverted self.

4.2 Freelancing and Entrepreneurship for Introverts

The entrepreneurial landscape brims with bold personalities, constant networking, and the pressure to be "always on." For introverts, this can feel like a daunting terrain, a cacophony of extroverted energy demanding a relentless self-promotion that drains our reserves. But fear not, fellow introverts! The world of freelancing and entrepreneurship holds hidden gems perfectly suited to our quiet strengths, allowing us to carve our own success path, pave it with thoughtful planning, and illuminate it with the steady flame of our unique talents.

Building a Successful Freelance Career as an Introvert

- Leveraging Your Strengths: Introverts often possess valuable skills that translate beautifully to freelance success. Our meticulous attention to detail ensures high-quality work. Our deep thinking leads to creative solutions and strategic planning. And our exceptional listening skills allow us to build strong relationships with clients, fostering trust and loyalty.

- Finding Your Niche: Instead of trying to be everything to everyone, identify your specific skills and passions. Focus on a niche market where your expertise shines and your introverted strengths can be fully utilized. This allows you to build a strong reputation within a smaller community, attracting clients who appreciate your unique value proposition.

- Embrace the Power of Online Marketing: While networking events may not be your forte, the digital world offers a safe haven for introverts to build their presence. Utilize online platforms to showcase your work, connect with potential clients, and build a professional network at your own pace. Social media, content marketing, and online portfolio building can be powerful tools for introverted freelancers, allowing you to connect with your audience on your own terms.

- Mastering the Art of Client Communication: While face-to-face meetings may drain your energy, effective communication is still crucial for freelance success. Hone your written communication skills, crafting clear and concise proposals and emails that articulate your value and expertise. Utilize video conferencing platforms for essential meetings, and prepare well-structured presentations to deliver your message with confidence and impact.

- Setting Boundaries and Protecting Your Energy: Freelancing often blurs the lines between work and personal life. Establish clear boundaries to protect your introverted energy. Schedule dedicated work hours, communicate effectively with clients about availability, and don't be afraid to say "no" to projects that would compromise your well-being. Remember, a rested and energized introvert is a productive and successful freelancer.

Leading Teams Effectively Without Sacrificing Introverted Tendencies

- Choose the Right Team Structure: As your business grows and you hire employees, consider a team structure that caters to your introverted nature. Create smaller, focused teams where collaboration and communication are efficient and meaningful. Delegate tasks effectively, giving your team members autonomy and ownership, allowing you to focus on your strategic leadership role without constant interaction.

- Lead by Example and Inspiration: As an introvert, your leadership style will naturally be different from the extroverted ideal. Focus on leading by example, setting a high standard for work ethic, dedication, and thoughtful decision-making. Share your vision with your team, articulate your goals with clarity, and inspire them with your passion for the project. Remember, your quiet confidence and unwavering commitment can be powerful motivators, even without the need for constant pep talks and motivational speeches.

- Embrace Asynchronous Communication: Don't feel pressured to hold constant meetings or engage in endless group discussions. Utilize project management tools, internal messaging platforms, and email to communicate effectively with your team, allowing them to work at their own pace and contribute their best in ways that suit their individual styles.

- Build Strong Relationships: While you may not crave constant socializing, invest in building strong one-on-one relationships with your team members. Schedule regular check-ins, actively listen to their concerns, and provide constructive feedback in a supportive and encouraging manner. Foster an environment where open communication and mutual respect are valued, and your introverted leadership style will be seen as a strength that allows for personalized support and thoughtful decision-making.

Navigating Office Politics in Entrepreneurial Ventures

- Focus on Building Trust and Respect: Instead of engaging in gossip or power plays, focus on building trust and respect within your organization. Be transparent in your communication, make decisions based on merit and data, and treat everyone with fairness and professionalism. This approach will build a positive and productive work environment, minimizing the impact of office politics and allowing your introverted leadership style to shine.

- Seek Strategic Alliances: Identify key individuals within your organization who share your values and appreciate your leadership style. Build strategic alliances with mentors, advisors, or partners who can complement your introverted tendencies and provide guidance in areas where you might need support. These connections can offer valuable advice, open doors to new opportunities, and navigate the complexities of office politics in a way that aligns with your introverted nature.

- Know When to Speak Up: While avoiding unnecessary conflict is key, there will be times when speaking up is essential. If you witness unethical behavior, observe decisions that could harm the company, or see issues that need addressing, don't shy away from raising your voice. Do so in a calm and reasoned manner, focusing on facts and solutions rather than emotions or personal attacks. Remember, your introverted nature, when coupled with thoughtful communication, can make your voice even more impactful when it does resonate.

- Building Your Support System: As an introvert navigating the world of entrepreneurship, having a strong support system is crucial. Surround yourself with like-minded individuals who understand your challenges and appreciate your strengths. These could be mentors, partners, colleagues, or friends who provide understanding, encouragement, and valuable advice. Remember, you don't have to navigate this life alone. A strong support system can help you recharge, overcome challenges, and celebrate your successes, fostering a sense of well-being and resilience that will propel you forward on your entrepreneurial path.

Introverts can not only thrive in the world of freelancing and entrepreneurship, but they can also bring unique and valuable strengths to these endeavors. By leveraging their strengths, building strategic alliances, and staying true to their nature, introverted entrepreneurs can create successful and fulfilling ventures, proving that leadership comes in many forms, and quiet confidence can be the most powerful tool in navigating the often-turbulent waters of office politics.

4.3 Personal Growth in Introverted Pursuits

The path to personal growth often conjures images of bustling seminars, high-energy networking events, and extroverted gurus preaching the loudest lessons. Yet, for introverts, this path lies less in the external noise and more in the fertile soil of inward reflection, deep engagement, and the pursuit of passions that resonate with our unique nature.

Harnessing the Power of Introverted Traits for Personal Growth

- The Gift of Deep Listening: Introverts excel at attuning to the subtle inner melodies, listening to their thoughts, feelings, and needs with an attentiveness that often eludes extroverts. This skill becomes a potent tool for self-awareness, providing insight into your motivations, desires, and the values that truly drive you. Cultivate this internal listening through journaling, meditation, or solitary walks in nature, allowing your introverted nature to guide you towards deeper self-understanding.

- The Strength of Quiet Reflection: In a world obsessed with constant action, introverts possess the invaluable ability to step back and reflect. Use this time to analyze your experiences, learn from mistakes, and envision your future goals with clarity. Journaling, creating vision boards, or simply spending time in quiet contemplation allows you to process information, refine your aspirations, and chart a course aligned with your authentic self.

- The Power of Creative Exploration: Introverts often channel their inner world into creative pursuits. Embrace your artistic inclinations, whether it's writing, painting, playing music, or crafting. Use these outlets to explore your emotions, express your unique perspective, and connect with your inner self on a deeper level. Remember, creativity thrives in solitude, and your introverted nature can give birth to original and meaningful expressions.

- The Value of Independent Learning: Introverts often prefer self-directed learning, absorbing knowledge through books, online courses, or independent research. Utilize this natural inclination to expand your horizons, delve into subjects that ignite your curiosity, and acquire skills that empower your personal growth. Remember, introverted learning is not a passive pursuit; it's an active exploration of your intellectual passions, fueled by your inherent desire for knowledge and understanding.

Pursuing Meaningful Work Aligned with Personal Values

- Identifying Your Values: Before embarking on any career path, take time to identify your core values. What matters most to you? Creativity, autonomy, intellectual challenge, social impact? Aligning your work with these values is crucial for introverted fulfillment, creating a sense of purpose that transcends external validation or societal expectations.

- Exploring Non-Traditional Paths: Don't be confined by conventional career narratives. Introverts often thrive in independent work, remote positions, or entrepreneurial ventures that offer flexibility, autonomy, and a quieter work environment. Research unconventional career options, such as freelance writing, online teaching, or data analysis, and explore possibilities that cater to your introverted needs while fulfilling your professional aspirations.

- Building a Trusted Network: While solo work has its advantages, introverts can still benefit from a supportive network. Seek out like-minded individuals, online communities, or professional associations that share your values and interests. These connections can provide valuable advice, encouragement, and a sense of belonging, mitigating the potential isolation of independent work.

- Prioritizing Self-Care: Introverts often find their energy depleted by constant interaction and demanding work environments. Prioritize self-care to maintain your well-being and prevent burnout. Schedule regular time for solitude, engage in activities that recharge your introverted batteries, and set healthy boundaries to protect your energy resources. Remember, a well-rested and energized introvert is a productive and fulfilled individual.

Balancing Ambition with Introverted Introspection

- Setting Realistic Goals: Introverts may be less prone to public displays of ambition, but that doesn't mean they lack aspirations. Set realistic and achievable goals for yourself, focusing on internal motivation and personal growth rather than external validation or public recognition. Celebrate your milestones, both big and small, and acknowledge your progress along the way.

- Embracing Introverted Ambition: Introverted ambition manifests differently than the extroverted version. Instead of seeking constant recognition, your drive may lie in mastering a skill, perfecting a craft, or contributing to a cause you deeply value. Focus on intrinsic rewards, the satisfaction of a job well done, and the joy of personal growth. Remember, your introverted ambition is just as powerful as any other, driving you towards meaningful contributions and personal fulfillment.

- Prioritizing Long-Term Vision: While extroverts may thrive in the fast-paced world of short-term goals and immediate rewards, introverts often excel in long-term planning and strategic thinking. Utilize your introverted tendencies to envision your future, develop a roadmap for achieving your goals, and make thoughtful decisions that pave the way for a future aligned with your introverted values and aspirations. Remember, your quiet ambition, fueled by thoughtful reflection and strategic planning, can lay the foundation for a lasting sense of accomplishment and a life filled with genuine meaning.

Finding success and personal growth as an introvert isn't about mimicking an extroverted ideal. It's about harnessing the power of your quiet strengths, nurturing your intrinsic motivations, and charting a path that resonates with your introverted nature. By listening to your inner voice, pursuing meaningful work, and balancing ambition with introspective wisdom, you can cultivate a life filled with fulfillment, purpose, and unique success, proving that the introverted personality, though quieter, can lead to just as spectacular destinations.

Chapter 5: Building Introvert Confidence

5.1 Building Introvert Confidence: Embracing Your Quiet Strength

The path to success, especially for introverts, is rarely a straight, sun-drenched highway. It's often a winding path, dappled with shadows and shrouded in self-doubt. Imposter syndrome whispers in our ears, painting us as fraudulent imposters masquerading as competent individuals. Fear of judgment looms like a storm cloud, threatening to drown out our voices and talents.

Unmasking the Sources of Self-Doubt

1. The Extroverted Ideal: Society often paints success with an extroverted brush. The loud, the outgoing, the life of the party – these are the archetypes of achievement. This constant bombardment can lead introverts to internalize a false narrative, questioning their own worth and capabilities simply because they don't fit the mold.

2. The Comparison Trap: Social media, brimming with curated highlight reels, fuels the flames of comparison. Seeing extroverts effortlessly navigating social landscapes and achieving recognition can leave introverts feeling inadequate, their introverted strengths seemingly invisible and undervalued.

3. The Imposter Syndrome: A persistent feeling of fraudulence, a nagging belief that you don't belong or deserve your success, is a common companion for

introverts. This imposter syndrome can paralyze potential, leading to self-sabotage and underachievement.

Confronting the Whispers of Self-Doubt

Self-doubt often thrives in the shadows of negative comparisons, societal expectations, and internalized narratives. Identify the root cause. Does it stem from comparing your introverted style to the extroverted ideal? Is it fueled by societal bias against quiet confidence? Or does it whisper from past experiences of judgment? Recognizing the source empowers you to challenge its validity.

After found out the root cause, that is the time to address it carefully. Our inner critic often turns into a harsh taskmaster, magnifying flaws and minimizing achievements. Counter its negativity with evidence of your strengths. List your accomplishments, big and small, highlighting your unique skills and valuable contributions. Celebrate each milestone, each hurdle overcome, each moment where your introverted qualities shone through. Remember, self-compassion is a powerful weapon against self-doubt.

Instead of letting the self-doubt narrative control the story, rewrite it. Replace negative narratives with affirmations that resonate with your introverted nature. "I thrive in focused environments" instead of "I'm not good at multitasking." "My thoughtful approach leads to well-planned solutions" instead of "I'm slow to make decisions."

This reframing empowers you to reclaim your personal narrative and build confidence from within.

Demystifying Imposter Syndrome

Imposter syndrome is a sneaky foe, masking self-worth with feelings of inadequacy and undeserved success. Recognize its common symptoms: attributing achievements to luck, downplaying expertise, and fearing exposure as a fraud. Remember, these feelings are experienced by countless successful individuals, regardless of personality type.

When imposter syndrome rears its ugly head, counter its claims with facts. Analyze your skills, knowledge, and experience. Recall situations where you demonstrated competence and leadership. Look for patterns of success, not just isolated instances of luck. Challenge the imposter's voice with evidence of your worth.

Don't go it alone. Confide in trusted friends, mentors, or even a therapist. Sharing your imposter feelings can validate your experience and provide valuable support. Seek guidance from others who understand the introverted perspective and can offer strategies for overcoming self-doubt. Remember, vulnerability can be a source of strength and connection.

Navigating the Fear of Judgment

Introverts are naturally attuned to social dynamics, often hyperaware of potential judgment. This can lead to hesitation in voicing opinions, participating in social events, or pursuing professional opportunities. Acknowledge this fear, but don't let it become a master manipulator.

Remember, your introverted perspective deserves to be heard. Practice articulating your thoughts in safe spaces, like with trusted friends or in writing. Join online communities of introverts where you can share your ideas and receive supportive feedback. Slowly build your confidence in expressing yourself in public settings.

You have the right to manage your energy and protect yourself from overwhelming situations. Learn to say no to social events that drain your batteries. Prioritize alone time for your introverted needs. Remember, setting boundaries isn't a sign of weakness but a reflection of self-respect and a sustainable approach to success. Don't be confined by societal definitions of success that equate it with constant interaction and outward validation. Forge your own path to fulfillment, one that prioritizes your introverted needs and celebrates your strengths. Define success on your own terms – whether it's mastering a skill, making a meaningful impact, or simply thriving in a way that aligns with your authentic self.

Building introvert confidence not a short term work. There will be setbacks and stumbles, but with each challenge overcome, your inner voice will grow stronger, your self-belief will deepen, and you'll discover the quiet power of introverted confidence. Embrace your unique strengths, silence the voices of doubt, and step into the world with the unshakeable conviction that you are capable, valuable, and worthy of success, on your own introverted terms.

5.2 Building Introvert Confidence

Confidence. That elusive quality often painted in vibrant colors of extroverted energy, booming voices, and a constant thirst for social interaction. For introverts, navigating this landscape can feel like venturing into a foreign country, where the customs and expectations seem alien, and the pressure to conform to a different rhythm threatens to drown our own quiet strength. Yet, within the introverted soul lies a hidden wellspring of confidence, waiting to be tapped.

Embracing Introverted Qualities as Sources of Strength

- Reframing Our Traits: Instead of viewing your introversion as a deficiency, recognize it as a distinct set of strengths. Your inherent attentiveness translates to deep listening skills, allowing you to truly understand others' needs and perspectives. Your thoughtful nature leads to meticulous planning and strategic thinking, ensuring your actions are well-informed and deliberate. And your preference for introspection empowers you to develop a profound self-awareness, a clear understanding of your values and goals. These are not weaknesses to overcome, but pillars of strength to build upon.

- Celebrating Quiet Confidence: Introverted confidence whispers, not shouts. It manifests in quiet determination, unwavering focus, and the quiet satisfaction of a job well done. It's the confidence that stems from internal validation, from knowing your worth isn't tied to external validation or the noise of the crowd. Embrace this intrinsic confidence, celebrate your unique way of radiating quiet strength, and let it guide your life to success.

- Leveraging Our Strengths in Social Settings: While social situations may drain your energy, introverts can still navigate them with confidence. Focus on quality over quantity, choosing interactions that are meaningful and engaging. Hone your active listening skills, ask insightful questions, and contribute thoughtful observations. Remember, it's not about being the loudest voice in the room, but about adding your unique value to the conversation, leaving a lasting impression through your quiet depth and introspective insights.

Developing a Positive Self-Image as an Introvert

Society often bombards us with implicit (and sometimes explicit) messages that equate introversion with social awkwardness or lack of ambition. Challenge these negative narratives with counter-evidence. Remind yourself of your successes, your strengths, and the unique value you bring to the world. Highlight the positive aspects of your introverted nature – your focus, your creativity, your deep thinking –

and cultivate a self-image that is rooted in self-acceptance and appreciation.

Find inspiration in successful introverts who have blazed their own paths. From writers and artists to CEOs and scientists, many remarkable individuals have achieved greatness while staying true to their introverted nature. Read their stories, learn from their experiences, and allow their confidence to ignite your own. Remember, you are not alone on this path; there is a vibrant community of introverts paving the way for success, each in their own unique and powerful way.

As introverts, we can be our own harshest critics. We dwell on perceived social missteps, compare ourselves to extroverted ideals, and amplify our shortcomings in the quiet chambers of our minds. Cultivate self-compassion instead. Practice forgiveness for your "social flaws," celebrate your successes both big and small, and treat yourself with the same kindness and understanding you would extend to a loved one.

Building Introvert Confidence Through Intentional Actions

The first step on the path to building confidence is shifting your internal narrative. Instead of dwelling on self-doubt, cultivate self-awareness. Take time to reflect on your strengths, talents, and accomplishments. Make a list, tangible evidence of your worth and capabilities. This isn't about bragging; it's about acknowledging your inherent value, a foundation upon which genuine confidence can be built.

Introverts often fall into the trap of striving for perfection, leading to disappointment and frustration. Remember, progress, not perfection, is the key to building confidence. Celebrate your small victories, no matter how seemingly insignificant. Aced that presentation? Completed a challenging project? Acknowledge your achievement, pat yourself on the back (figuratively, of course), and let the satisfaction of progress fuel your self-belief.

While introverts thrive in their comfort zones, stepping outside them occasionally can be a powerful confidence booster. Choose activities that stretch your social muscles but don't drain your energy. Join a book club, attend a workshop related to your interests, or volunteer for a cause you care about. These small steps in unfamiliar territory can reveal hidden strengths and expose you to new perspectives, all while building confidence in your ability to navigate beyond your introverted haven. Remember, your quiet voice, your thoughtful demeanor, and your measured approach are valuable assets. Don't try to be someone you're not. Instead, hone your communication skills in ways that resonate with your introverted nature. Write impactful emails, craft concise presentations, and prioritize active listening, becoming a master of meaningful communication, not just loud proclamations.

Building introverted confidence is a gradual process, a quiet rebellion against a world that often misunderstands introverted strengths. By implementing these strategies, prioritizing self-care, and celebrating your unique voice, you can pave the way for a future where introverted confidence isn't just a possibility, it's your reality. Remember, the world needs the thoughtful wisdom, the insightful analysis, and the unwavering dedication of introverts. Let your quiet strength become your beacon, lighting the path to success, on your own terms.

5.3 Authenticity in the Professional World

In the boisterous arena of professional life, where extroversion seems to hold the microphone and command the spotlight, introverts often face a silent struggle. The pressure to conform, to embrace a persona of effortless networking and constant self-promotion, can create a dissonance between who we are and who we feel we "should" be. But what if the key to success lies not in mimicking another, but in embracing the quiet power of our own introverted authenticity?

Staying True to Introverted Values in Professional Settings

- Understanding Your Core Values: Before crafting your professional persona, take time to identify the values that anchor your introverted self. Perhaps you cherish meaningful connections over fleeting acquaintances, deep reflection over constant chatter, or focused work over social whirlwinds. Aligning your work life with these values fuels internal fulfillment and ensures your career path resonates with your authentic self.

- Embracing Introverted Strengths: Instead of viewing your introverted tendencies as weaknesses to minimize, recognize them as powerful assets. Your exceptional listening skills allow you to truly hear and understand colleagues. Your deep thinking facilitates strategic problem-solving and informed decision-making. Your thoughtful communication ensures clarity and precision in your messages. Embrace these strengths, and watch them become pillars of your professional success.

- Setting Boundaries to Protect Your Energy: Introverts require solitude to recharge their batteries. Don't apologize for needing quiet time or declining after-work events that drain your energy. Set clear boundaries, communicate your needs effectively, and prioritize activities that replenish your introverted reservoir. Remember, a well-rested and energized introvert is a more productive and successful professional.

Building an Authentic Professional Persona

Introverts often underestimate the power of their voice. Hone your communication skills, crafting your messages with care and confidence. Articulate your ideas clearly, both in writing and during meetings. Remember, well-delivered presentations and impactful proposals don't require theatrics, but rather a clear understanding of your subject matter and the unwavering conviction of your introspective insights.

While extroverts may excel at small talk, introverts possess a unique talent for crafting compelling narratives. Use storytelling to connect with colleagues and clients, sharing your expertise through case studies, insightful anecdotes, or well-constructed presentations. Your ability to weave a captivating narrative around data and information can leave a lasting impression, showcasing your introverted strengths in a powerful and engaging way.

Surround yourself with individuals who appreciate and complement your introverted nature. Find mentors who understand the power of quiet confidence and can guide you through the professional landscape. Connect with colleagues who share your work ethic and value thoughtful collaboration. These strategic alliances create a supportive network that amplifies your voice and empowers you to navigate the extroverted world without compromising your authenticity.

Navigating External Expectations Without Compromising Authenticity

Introverts often face stereotypes about lacking leadership potential or being unsocial. Actively challenge these misconceptions by demonstrating your strengths. Showcase your insightful decision-making, inspiring leadership by example, and building strong, meaningful connections with colleagues. Let your accomplishments speak louder than any preconceived notions, proving that introverts can thrive in leadership roles and professional settings.

Embrace a different leadership style. Lead by inspiring a shared vision, by fostering thoughtful collaboration, and by creating a work environment that values deep thinking and focused execution. Remember, effective leadership doesn't require constant charisma or boisterous pronouncements. Introverted leaders can inspire through quiet confidence, meticulous planning, and unwavering commitment to excellence.

Don't feel pressured to conform to every expectation. Learn to say "no" with grace and clarity. Explain your decision politely, offer alternative solutions if possible, and avoid feeling guilty for prioritizing your introverted needs. Setting healthy boundaries doesn't make you less dedicated or professional; it demonstrates your self-awareness and your commitment to personal well-being, both crucial for introverted success.

Authenticity is not about perfection. It's about embracing your introverted self, flaws and all, and presenting a genuine version of yourself that resonates with your values and strengths. The professional world may seem dominated by extroverted voices, but your introverted voice is powerful, nuanced, and capable of achieving remarkable things. Embrace your quiet confidence, stay true to your authentic self, and watch your unique brand of success unfold.

Chapter 6: Cultivating Introvert Joy

6.1 The Benefits of Being an Introvert

In a world that celebrates the loud, the gregarious, the life-of-the-party, it's easy for introverts to feel their quiet nature as a hidden liability. But what if we reframed the narrative? What if we embraced the unique benefits of our introversion, seeing it not as a deficiency, but as a wellspring of joy, richness, and connection?

Embracing the Joy of Deep Reflection

Introverts possess an inherent gift – the ability to step back from the constant hustle and bustle, enter the sanctuary of their minds, and engage in deep reflection. This introspective capacity isn't merely idle daydreaming; it's a powerful tool for self-discovery, growth, and ultimately, joy.

Imagine, for a moment, a sculptor meticulously studying a block of marble, envisioning the masterpiece waiting to be born. The sculptor doesn't rush, doesn't seek the applause of the crowd. Instead, they delve into the intricacies of the stone, understanding its grain, its texture, its potential. Introverts are like that sculptor, carving their own masterpieces of self-awareness through reflection.

This introspection allows us to delve into our emotions, analyze our experiences, and understand our motivations on a deeper level. We can ponder complex ideas, grapple with philosophical questions, and engage in intellectual pursuits that bring genuine satisfaction, untouched by the need for external validation. In the quiet hum of introspection, we discover our authentic selves, our values, and our passions, laying the foundation for a life aligned with our true nature.

Furthermore, introverts are gifted with a keen sense of observation. We notice the subtle nuances in human behavior, the unspoken emotions that flicker across faces, the hidden stories woven into the tapestry of everyday interactions. This observational skill allows us to connect with others on a deeper level, building meaningful relationships based on empathy and understanding. We become the confidantes, the listeners, the individuals who offer unwavering support and insightful advice, enriching the lives of those around us in a way that transcends the noise and superficiality of the extroverted world.

Nurturing Rich Inner Lives as Introverts

Our introversion isn't a void, a lack of something; it's a potent source of inner richness. While extroverts may thrive in the constant stimulation of external stimuli, introverts find solace and joy in the vibrant world within. We are the architects of our own internal landscapes, cultivating creativity, imagination, and a deep appreciation for the beauty and complexity of the human experience.

Imagine, for a moment, a hidden garden, untouched by the harsh sun, thriving in the cool shade of introspection. This is the garden of the introverted mind, where imagination takes root, nurtured by solitude and silence. We are the storytellers, the artists, the musicians who weave tales, paint emotions, and compose melodies that resonate with the depths of our being. Our inner world becomes a sanctuary, a refuge where we can explore our passions, express ourselves freely, and find solace in the quiet hum of our own creativity.

This inner richness spills over into our external interactions. We bring thoughtful perspectives to conversations, offering unique insights that stem from our deep reflections and imaginative explorations. We are the creators of innovative solutions, the problem-solvers who see beyond the surface, drawing inspiration from the hidden depths of our minds. In a world that often values speed and immediacy, introverts offer the invaluable gift of slow, thoughtful consideration, enriching our collective experience with depth and nuance.

Fostering Meaningful Relationships Based on Introverted Values

Introverts may not crave the constant buzz of large social gatherings, but we are not loners. We crave deep, meaningful connections, built on shared values, mutual respect, and genuine understanding. We invest our energy in cultivating a small circle of trusted friends, individuals who appreciate our quiet nature and reciprocate our introverted values.

Imagine, for a moment, a circle of stones, carefully chosen and arranged, forming a strong and stable foundation. This is the circle of an introvert's relationships, built on trust, shared values, and authentic connection. We are the loyal friends, the confidantes who offer a listening ear and a nonjudgmental space. We are the companions who engage in meaningful conversations, delve into deep topics, and find joy in the quiet intimacy of shared understanding.

Our introverted nature allows us to cultivate relationships based on genuine connection rather than superficiality. We invest time in understanding our loved ones, offering empathy, support, and unwavering loyalty. These deep bonds become a source of strength and joy, a refuge from the noise of the world where we can truly be ourselves and find acceptance and appreciation for our unique way of being.

Introversion isn't a deficit, it's a treasure. It's a gift that allows us to experience the world in a unique way, and make it as our strength to pave a way to joyful life. So, start embrace your treasure and steps on path to a better life.

6.2 Creating a Fulfilling Lifestyle

For many introverts, the pursuit of joy can feel like a treasure hunt in a land designed for extroverts. Loud restaurants throb with overwhelming energy, social calendars overflow with draining obligations, and the relentless pressure to "be on" threatens to extinguish our inner flame. But amidst the external cacophony, there exists a tranquil oasis reserved for those who cherish quiet contemplation and savor the subtle pleasures of solitude: the introverted haven of joy.

Prioritizing Activities that Align with Introverted Needs

Introverts recharge their batteries in solitude and find rejuvenation in activities that engage their minds and stimulate their senses in a measured way. Prioritizing these activities becomes the cornerstone of a fulfilling lifestyle.

1. Embrace Solitude as a Recharge Station: Remember, introverts flourish in periods of solitude. Prioritize activities that replenish your energy reserves, whether it's losing yourself in a captivating book, immersing yourself in nature's embrace, or indulging in the quietude of a solo creative pursuit. Don't let societal pressures to socialize constantly deplete your introverted battery; schedule alone time into your day with the same reverence you'd show any vital appointment.

2. Seek Activities that Speak to Your Soul: Introverts often find joy in activities that stimulate their minds and ignite their passions. Dive into the captivating world of online courses, explore historical archives, or delve into the intricacies of a new skill. Embrace activities that allow you to learn, discover, and create at your own pace, without the need for external validation or a cheering audience.

3. Connect with Like-Minded Souls: While solitude plays a crucial role, introverts also crave meaningful connections. Seek out communities, online or offline, where you can engage with others who share your interests and understand your introverted nature. Whether it's a book club for fellow bibliophiles, an online forum for passionate artisans, or a hiking group that thrives on quiet contemplation, surround

yourself with people who appreciate your introspective nature and enrich your world without draining your energy.

4. Redefine "Socializing": For introverts, socializing doesn't have to translate to large, boisterous gatherings. Cultivate meaningful connections through one-on-one conversations, intimate dinner parties with close friends, or virtual meetings with fellow enthusiasts. Remember, quality trumps quantity, and meaningful conversations held in quiet corners can leave a far deeper imprint than fleeting exchanges in crowded rooms.

Building a Daily Routine that Nurtures Introverted Tendencies

Structure can be a friend to introverts, providing a sense of stability and predictability while allowing you to prioritize activities that align with your needs. Consider these tips:

1. Listen to Your Body's Rhythms: Introverts often experience dips in energy throughout the day. Schedule demanding tasks during your peak energy hours and leave time for quiet contemplation and self-care during your low periods. This awareness of your natural rhythms allows you to structure your day for optimal productivity and well-being.

2. Create Boundaries and Manage Social Energy: Introverts can feel drained by excessive social interaction. Set clear boundaries, politely decline invitations that feel overwhelming, and communicate your need for solitude to friends and family. Remember, prioritizing your introverted

needs is not selfish; it's essential for maintaining your energy and preventing burnout.

3. Craft a Sanctuary in Your Home: Create a space in your home that feels like your own personal haven. Fill it with things that bring you comfort and joy, whether it's a cozy reading nook, a quiet corner for writing, or a well-lit desk for creative pursuits. This sanctuary becomes a refuge where you can retreat to recharge, reconnect with yourself, and experience the simple joy of being in your own company.

4. Embrace Rituals and Routines: Small, consistent rituals can bring a sense of peace and stability to an introverted life. Develop a morning routine that sets the tone for the day, an evening ritual that helps you unwind, or a weekly activity that you look forward to with anticipation. These rituals provide a sense of grounding and comfort, adding pockets of joy to your daily experience.

Finding Joy in the Simplicity of Introverted Pleasures

Introverts derive profound joy from simple pleasures that resonate with their introspective nature. Appreciating and incorporating these subtle joys into daily life transforms routine activities into meaningful moments.

1. The Delights of Solo Pursuits: Don't underestimate the joy found in solitary activities. Curl up with a good book, indulge in a quiet movie marathon, or lose yourself in a challenging puzzle. Introverts often find immense pleasure

in activities that allow them to focus their attention and immerse themselves in their own company. Remember, alone time is not loneliness; it is an opportunity for self-discovery and quiet enjoyment.

2. The Art of Savoring Small Moments: Train yourself to appreciate the little things. Take pleasure in the warmth of a cup of tea, the scent of a freshly baked loaf of bread, or the intricate beauty of a snowflake. Introverts excel at noticing and appreciating the subtle nuances of life, and cultivating this mindful approach can transform ordinary moments into sources of joy.

3. The Magic of Meaningful Connections: While introverts may prefer smaller, more intimate gatherings, the connections they forge are often deep and lasting. Invest in cultivating close relationships with like-minded individuals who understand and appreciate your introverted nature. Share meaningful conversations, engage in intellectual discussions, or simply enjoy each other's quiet presence. Remember, quality over quantity is the mantra of introverted joy, and genuine connection trumps fleeting social interactions.

Cultivating introverted joy is not about isolating yourself from the world, but about crafting a life that nurtures your unique needs and celebrates your inner strengths. By embracing your introverted essence, you can build a haven of joy within the whirlwind of an extroverted world. Let your joy become a beacon, illuminating the path for other introverts seeking happiness on their own terms.

6.3 Mindfulness and Introversion

For introverts, navigating the constant stimulation of modern life can feel like walking a tightrope blindfolded. Our need for solitude and introspection clashes with the extroverted ideals of constant activity and external validation. This often leads to stress, overwhelm, and a disconnect from our own inner joy.

Why is Mindfulness so Crucial for Introverts?

Our sensitive natures, while enriching our experiences, can also leave us susceptible to stress and overstimulation. The constant influx of information, the demands of social interaction, and the pressure to conform to extroverted ideals can drain our energy and leave us feeling depleted. Mindfulness offers a powerful antidote, equipping us with tools to manage stress, cultivate calm, and reconnect with the richness of our inner world.

While mindfulness may seem like an extrovert's playground, introverts possess inherent strengths that make them natural allies in this practice. Our quiet attentiveness, introspective nature, and capacity for deep reflection create a fertile ground for cultivating awareness and appreciating the nuances of our inner world. Think of it like this: extroverts are drawn to the fireworks outside, while introverts hold the spark that can ignite a dazzling inner display.

Stress Management Tailored for Introverts

Stress, however, can dim that inner spark. The constant bombardment of external stimuli, even positive ones, can drain our introverted batteries. To prevent burnout and cultivate joy, we need stress management techniques tailored to our needs. Here are some effective strategies:

- Embrace Solitary Recharge: Don't feel obligated to attend every social event or fill every spare moment with external activity. Schedule regular time for solitude, be it a solo walk in nature, a cozy reading session, or simply enjoying a quiet cup of tea in your sanctuary. These moments of solitude allow you to replenish your energy reserves and reconnect with your inner self.

- Master the Art of "No": Don't be afraid to say "no" to requests that drain your energy or compromise your need for alone time. Setting healthy boundaries and prioritizing your well-being isn't selfish, it's essential for maintaining your introverted balance.

- Mindful Breathing: When stress threatens to overwhelm, simple breathing exercises can be your anchor. Practice mindful breathing, focusing on the rhythm of your inhale and exhale. This calms the mind, grounds you in the present moment, and releases tension built up in your body.

- Creative Expression: Introverts often find catharsis and stress relief through creative pursuits. Whether it's journaling, painting, playing music, or simply crafting, let your creative juices flow. This allows you to process emotions, explore your inner world, and find joy in the act of creation itself.

Integrating Mindfulness into Daily Life

Mindfulness isn't about achieving some zen-like state of constant calm. It's about cultivating awareness of your thoughts, feelings, and bodily sensations in the present moment. The good news is, you can integrate mindfulness into your daily life in simple, but impactful ways:

- Mindful Mornings: Start your day with a few minutes of mindful breathing or gentle stretching. This sets the tone for a more conscious and present day, allowing you to approach experiences with greater clarity and calmness.

- Mindful Eating: Instead of mindlessly scrolling through your phone while eating, savor your food. Pay attention to the flavors, textures, and even the aroma of your meal. This not only promotes mindful eating habits but also helps you appreciate the simple pleasures of everyday life.

- Mindful Movement: Introverts often underestimate the power of movement. Incorporate mindful walks, yoga, or gentle stretching into your routine. Focus on the sensations in your body as you move, and observe the connection between your breath and movement.

- Mindful Technology Use: In our digital age, constant notifications and screen time can easily hijack our attention. Set boundaries around technology use, scheduling screen-free times and practicing mindful technology engagement. When you do use your devices, be present and avoid mindlessly scrolling or multitasking.

Cultivating introvert joy is not about forcing yourself to be someone you're not. It's about embracing your introverted nature, honoring your needs for quiet and solitude, and finding ways to nourish your inner world. By integrating mindfulness into your daily life, you can create a sanctuary of peace within, allowing your unique strengths and perspectives to shine in a world that desperately needs them.

Chapter 7: Financial Success for Introverts

7.1 Budgeting Strategies Aligned with Introvert Preferences

Financial planning often gets painted in bold colors, demanding constant tracking, boisterous goal setting, and a relentless pursuit of "more." But for many introverts, this extroverted approach to finances can feel like a cacophony, draining their energy and pushing them away from the mindful budgeting practices that lead to true financial success.

Developing Personalized Budget Plans for Introverts

Gone are the days of cookie-cutter budgets that force introverted needs into extroverted molds. This is your call to create a financial plan that reflects your values, prioritizes your well-being, and fuels your introverted strengths. Here's how you can craft your unique blueprint:

- Embrace Introspection: Instead of copying cookie-cutter budgets, dive deep into your own needs and values. Ask yourself: What truly brings me joy? What experiences are worth sacrificing for? What are my long-term goals, and how can my budget support them? This introspective approach ensures your financial decisions are aligned with your authentic self, not societal expectations.

- Focus on Quality, Not Quantity: Introverts often crave deep connections and meaningful experiences over fleeting pleasures. Translate this preference into your budget by prioritizing quality over quantity. Invest in experiences that enrich your life, like learning a new skill, traveling to a destination that resonates with you, or attending a small, intimate event with like-minded individuals.

- Prioritize Sustainability over Splurges: The introverted need for stability and security can be reflected in your financial habits. Focus on building a sustainable financial foundation, prioritizing long-term goals like retirement savings or debt repayment over impulsive splurges. Remember, small, consistent steps lead to lasting financial peace, creating a haven of calm amidst the external noise.

- Embrace Minimalism: The introverted preference for simplicity can translate beautifully into financial minimalism. Declutter your spending habits, identify unnecessary expenses, and streamline your budget to focus on what truly matters. This creates a sense of mental clarity and control, allowing you to invest your resources in experiences and passions that nourish your soul.

Prioritizing Experiences over Material Possessions in Financial Planning

Achieving financial success as an introvert is not about conforming to an extroverted ideal; it's about building a system that works for you. Here are some key takeaways to guide your planning:

- Invest in Memories, Not Possessions: Introverts often find greater joy in experiences than material possessions. Allocate a portion of your budget towards experiences, be it a solo hike in nature, a cozy weekend getaway with a close friend, or a class that ignites your curiosity. These investments create lasting memories and personal growth, enriching your life far beyond the fleeting satisfaction of material acquisitions.

- Seek Out Shared Experiences: Introverts may prefer smaller, more intimate gatherings, but that doesn't mean they shy away from connection. Budget for shared experiences that nurture your relationships, like hosting a potluck dinner for close friends, attending a local art exhibition with a partner, or joining a book club focused on your favorite author. These shared moments deepen connections and foster a sense of belonging, enriching your life without the need for extravagant social outings.

- Invest in Personal Growth: Introverts often crave self-discovery and intellectual exploration. Budget for experiences that fuel your personal growth, such as attending workshops, online courses, or investing in books and resources that expand your knowledge and skills. These investments in yourself not only enrich your life but also have the potential to open doors to future opportunities and career advancement, all while aligning with your introverted need for solitude and introspection.

Utilizing Online Tools and Automation for Financial Management

Technology can be a powerful ally for introverted financial management. Embrace online tools and automated systems to minimize social interaction and streamline your processes. Here are some options to consider:

- Embrace Technology as a Time-Saving Ally: Introverts often value their time and energy. Utilize online budgeting tools and financial apps to automate tasks, track expenses, and analyze your spending patterns. This not only simplifies financial management but also frees up your mental space for activities that nourish your introverted soul.

- Prioritize Security and Privacy: While technology offers convenience, introverts may prioritize privacy and data security. Choose reputable financial tools with strong security protocols and be mindful of the information you share online. Remember, your financial data is a personal sanctuary; safeguard it with the same care you give to your inner world.

- Find Tools that Align with Your Preferences: The plethora of financial tools can be overwhelming. Research and choose apps and platforms that cater to your introverted preferences. Look for tools with simple interfaces, minimal notifications, and customized dashboards that provide insights without bombarding you with information overload.

- Utilize Automation for Effortless Progress: Leverage the power of automation to set and forget recurring bills, investments, and savings goals. This frees you from the constant mental burden of managing finances, allowing you to focus on your goals and aspirations with a renewed sense of clarity and peace.

By embracing your introverted preferences, prioritizing meaningful experiences, and utilizing technology strategically, you can craft a financial roadmap that leads to true success, not just in terms of numbers but also in terms of inner peace, personal growth, and a life filled with experiences that truly nourish your soul. Remember, financial success for introverts is not about replicating extroverted narratives; it's about building a financial haven which align with your values.

7.2 Building Wealth Without Extensive Networking

The world of wealth creation often paints a picture of boisterous networking events, packed conferences, and constant social interaction. For introverts, this can feel like a daunting landscape, a cacophony of extroverted energy that drains our reserves and leaves us yearning for the quiet sanctuary of introspection. But fear not, fellow introverts! Financial success is not a game reserved for the socially adept. In fact, our introverted strengths – our meticulous attention to detail, our deep analytical skills, and our comfort with independent learning – can be powerful tools for building wealth without compromising our natural inclinations.

Leveraging Online Platforms and Communities for Financial Education

Forget the pressure of crowded seminars and intimidating workshops. The internet offers a treasure trove of resources for introverts seeking financial knowledge. Online courses, educational blogs, and informative podcasts allow you to learn at your own pace, in the comfort of your own space. Explore platforms like Udemy, Coursera, and Khan Academy for comprehensive financial literacy courses, or delve into specialized topics on blogs like Mr. Money Mustache or The Financial Diet. Join online communities dedicated to specific financial goals, such as debt-free living or early retirement, where you can connect with like-minded individuals and learn from their experiences.

The beauty of online platforms lies in their accessibility and anonymity. You can absorb information at your own speed, ask questions without feeling judged, and avoid the overwhelming social pressure often associated with traditional financial education. This self-directed approach empowers you to tailor your learning steps to your specific needs and interests, creating a personalized roadmap to financial success.

Focusing on Niche Expertise Over Extensive Social Circles

The conventional wisdom of "it's not what you know, it's who you know" may not apply to introverts seeking financial success. While networking can be valuable, it doesn't have to be the sole driver of your financial plan.

Instead, cultivate a deep understanding of a specific niche, becoming an expert in a particular area of finance or investment. This could be anything from real estate investing to cryptocurrency trading, personal finance management to sustainable investing.

Focusing on a niche allows you to leverage your introverted strengths of research, analysis, and independent learning. You can delve into the intricacies of your chosen field, mastering the technical skills and market knowledge necessary for success. This expertise, coupled with your introverted dedication and focus, can become your competitive advantage, attracting clients and partners who value your specialized knowledge and meticulous approach. Remember, in the world of finance, depth trumps breadth. Build a fortress of expertise within your niche, and the right connections will naturally gravitate towards you.

Choosing Financial Advisors Attuned to Introverted Communication Styles

Seeking financial guidance doesn't require constant meetings and lengthy discussions. When choosing an advisor, prioritize their understanding of your introverted communication style. Look for someone who values clear, concise communication and respects your need for time and space to process information. An advisor who welcomes written communication, offers detailed reports, and engages in focused consultations can be a valuable partner for an introverted investor.

Don't hesitate to interview potential advisors before committing. Ask about their communication preferences, their approach to client interactions, and their willingness to accommodate your introverted needs. Remember, a good financial advisor should be a trusted confidante, not a social pressure cooker. Choose someone who understands your unique communication style and builds a relationship based on mutual respect and understanding.

Building wealth as an introvert is not about conforming to an extroverted ideal. It's about leveraging your strengths, embracing your natural inclinations, and crafting a financial plan that aligns with your personality and values. By utilizing online resources, cultivating niche expertise, and choosing the right financial advisor, you can navigate the world of finance with confidence and success, proving that introverts can not only achieve financial goals but excel in doing so on their own terms.

7.3 Introspective Thinking in Investing

In the high-octane world of finance, where headlines scream of overnight fortunes and market meltdowns, the introvert investor might feel like an outsider. Bombarded by loud claims, relentless advice, and the constant chatter of the financial news cycle, it's easy to succumb to the pressure to act, to chase the latest trend, and lose sight of your well-being and long-term goals. But fear not, fellow introverts! There exists a quieter, more deliberate path to financial success, one paved with deep research, thoughtful analysis, and a firm understanding of your own risk tolerance. This is the path of introspective investing, where your natural strengths become your secret weapons in navigating the financial landscape.

The Introvert's Advantage in Research and Analysis
Introverts are natural-born researchers. We gravitate towards quiet corners, dive deep into data, and relish the process of uncovering insights hidden beneath the surface. This inclination translates beautifully to the world of investing. While extroverts may thrive on quick decisions and gut instincts, introverts excel at deep research and meticulous analysis. This natural inclination becomes your greatest asset in the world of investing.

Before sinking your hard-earned money into any asset, dive into the research with the focused determination of a seasoned detective. Calmly analyze financial statements, analyze market trends, compare investment options with meticulous detail, and craft a personalized strategy based on our unique risk tolerance and goals. Don't be afraid to ask questions, seek out trusted resources, and challenge conventional wisdom. Remember, your introspective nature allows you to go beyond the surface and uncover hidden gems, building a strong foundation for informed investment decisions.

Embracing the Power of "Low-Touch" Investing

The extroverted ideal of the active trader, glued to screens and chasing adrenaline-fueled trades, is not a prerequisite for financial success. In fact, for introverts, a "low-touch" approach can be far more effective and stress-free. Consider index funds, diversified portfolios, and automated investment platforms. These strategies leverage the power of long-term market trends and diversification, minimizing the need for constant monitoring and impulsive decisions. You can reap the benefits of the market's growth while staying true to your introverted preference for quiet analysis and measured action.

Prioritizing Long-Term Goals over Social Pressure

Introverts are often less susceptible to the herd mentality and the fear of missing out that can drive impulsive financial decisions. We are more likely to prioritize our long-term goals, be it securing a comfortable retirement, building a solid college fund for your children, or achieving financial independence, over the fleeting allure of chasing quick gains or succumbing to social pressure from friends or family investing in the "next big thing." This allows us to stay on track with our carefully crafted plans, avoiding the emotional rollercoaster of short-term market fluctuations and the potential pitfalls of impulsive, uninformed decisions.

Building a Financial Strategy Aligned with Your Values

Financial success for introverts should not be about chasing someone else's definition of wealth. Instead, it's about aligning your financial strategy with your values and priorities. Do you value sustainability and ethical business practices? Explore socially responsible investment options. Do you prioritize financial security above all else? Focus on building a diversified portfolio with low risk and guaranteed returns. Do you dream of financial freedom to pursue your passions? Craft a plan that prioritizes early retirement or income-generating investments. Remember, your introspective nature allows you to connect with your deeper values and build a financial future that truly resonates with you.

Cultivating a Supportive Network

While introverts may favor solitude, building a supportive network of like-minded individuals can be invaluable in your financial plan. Seek out mentors, financial advisors who understand your introverted approach, or online communities of introverted investors. Sharing experiences, learning from others, and receiving objective advice can provide valuable insights and bolster your confidence as you navigate the financial landscape.

Finding Joy in the Process

Financial planning can easily become a chore, another item on the ever-growing to-do list. But for introverts, it can also be a source of intellectual stimulation and personal satisfaction. Embrace the research process, the thrill of uncovering hidden trends, and the satisfaction of building a solid financial foundation. Turn it into a quiet pursuit, a form of introspection that not only secures your future but also brings you a sense of accomplishment and control.

Introverts are not destined to be financial afterthoughts. Our quiet strength, analytical minds, and long-term focus are powerful tools in the world of investing. By embracing your introspective nature, prioritizing your values, and utilizing "low-touch" strategies, you can build a secure and fulfilling financial future without sacrificing your authentic self. So, step into the quiet corner, sharpen your analytical mind, and chart your own path to financial success, one thoughtful decision at a time.

Chapter 8: Career Success for Introverts

8.1 Identifying Introvert-Friendly Work Environments

For an introvert, the professional world can often resemble a bustling marketplace, with the loudest voices claiming the most prominent stalls. But amidst the clamour, a quieter path to career success exists, one paved with introspective wisdom, focused execution, and the unique strengths that introverted individuals possess.

Recognizing Introverted Qualities Before Choosing Your Path

Before embarking on your career path, take a moment to acknowledge the intrinsic strengths that define your introversion. Do you thrive in independent work, excelling at focused analysis and meticulous attention to detail? Do you possess exceptional listening skills, drawing insights from others and building deep, meaningful connections? Are you a creative powerhouse, channeling your inner world into innovative ideas and expressive projects? Recognizing these strengths is the first step towards identifying environments that will amplify your potential and allow you to flourish.

Here is guide to help you consider your career path :

- Deep-Thinking and Insight: Introverts possess the superpower of introspective analysis. They excel at delving into problems, unearthing hidden connections, and formulating well-considered solutions. Look for fields that value meticulous attention to detail, strategic planning, and creative problem-solving, where your contemplative nature can truly shine.

Independent Learning and Mastery: Introverts thrive in self-directed learning environments. They find their groove in research, independent studies, and continuous skill development. Choose careers that offer intellectual challenges, opportunities for autonomous learning, and the freedom to delve into specialized areas of knowledge.

- Strong Communication, Not Constant Conferencing: While introverts may prefer smaller social circles, their communication skills are often exceptional. They excel at listening intently, expressing themselves with clarity and precision, and fostering meaningful connections through in-depth conversations. Don't confuse preference for smaller interactions with a lack of communication prowess; seek roles that value thoughtful communication over constant chatter.

- Quiet Creativity and Innovation: Introverts often channel their inner world into creative expression. They excel in writing, design, artistic pursuits, and innovative problem-solving. Embrace careers that allow you to unleash your creative spark, whether it's through independent artistic endeavors or contributing your unique perspective to collaborative projects.

- Stamina for Focused Work: Introverts thrive in environments that allow them to dive deep into tasks without frequent interruptions. They possess the stamina for focused work, concentration, and producing high-quality output during sustained periods of solitude. Seek roles that value individual contributions, provide uninterrupted work time, and acknowledge the power of focused attention.

Introversion is not a weakness to overcome, but a set of powerful tools waiting to be wielded. Embrace your analytical mind, your independent spirit, and your love for deep thinking. These are the cornerstones upon which you'll build a career that resonates with your authentic self, a career where you can contribute meaningfully without sacrificing your introverted needs.

Strategic Roles that Align with Your Introverted Strengths

Now, let's translate your strengths into concrete career possibilities. Do you revel in the world of data and analysis? Consider roles like data scientist, research analyst, or librarian, where your introspective focus and meticulous attention to detail will shine. Are you drawn to creative exploration? Explore graphic design, writing, or music composition, where your inner world can blossom into tangible expressions. If your talents lie in communication, look for roles like technical writer, editor, or grant writer, where your ability to translate complex information into clear prose will be highly valued.

Let's explore specific career paths that resonate with the introverted spirit.

- Data Analyst: Dive deep into the world of numbers, patterns, and insights. Analyze data, uncover hidden trends, and formulate strategic recommendations, all while enjoying the solitude and focused work that fuels your introverted mind.

- Scientist or Researcher: Craft groundbreaking discoveries in the quiet laboratory of your own mind. Conduct independent research, delve into complex problems, and contribute to scientific advancements, all while thriving in the environment of focused inquiry that introverts adore.

- Writer or Editor: Let your introspective observations and masterful wordsmithing take center stage. Craft compelling narratives, edit with meticulous precision, and share your unique perspective with the world, all while enjoying the solitude and introspection that empowers your writing.

- Software Developer or Programmer: Build intricate digital worlds in the comfort of your own space. Code, create, and solve complex problems through the power of logic and creativity, all while enjoying the focused work and independent problem-solving that introverts crave.

- Designer or Graphic Artist: Breathe life into your inner vision through visual storytelling. Design stunning graphics, craft impactful interfaces, and express your unique aesthetic, all while enjoying the solitary creative process that allows your introverted creativity to flourish.

Remember, you're not limited to specific industries or titles. Introverted strengths can be valuable assets in virtually any field. The key is to identify roles that offer autonomy, intellectual challenge, and minimal constant interaction. Consider freelance work, online businesses, or remote positions that allow you to work on your own terms, recharge in solitude, and contribute on your own schedule.

Advocating for Remote Work Options and Flexible Schedules

Many traditional work environments are designed for the extroverted ideal, prioritizing open-plan offices, constant meetings, and endless social interaction. But don't be disheartened! The tide is turning towards greater workplace flexibility, and introverts are at the forefront of this shift. Embrace your voice and advocate for remote work options, flexible schedules, and quiet spaces within your organization. Highlight the benefits of introverted work styles, such as focused productivity, high-quality results, and well-considered solutions.

Advocating for your needs isn't selfish, it's empowering. By paving the way for introverted work styles, you're not just creating a more comfortable environment for yourself, but contributing to a more inclusive and diverse workplace for everyone.

By understanding your strengths, identifying suitable career paths, and advocating for your needs, you can carve out a successful and fulfilling career that honors your introverted nature. Remember, your quiet confidence, analytical mind, and independent spirit are valuable assets in the workplace. Don't be afraid to claim your rightful place and rewrite the narrative of introverted success, proving that quiet strength can lead to resounding achievements in any professional arena.

8.2 Navigating the Workplace

Introverts often face the misconception that effective workplace is synonymous with boisterous words and effortless small talk. But in workplace and meeting, the kind that builds bridges and fuels progress, is a nuanced art form, requiring not just volume, but depth, clarity, and a keen understanding of your audience. This is where your introverted strengths shine

Effective Communication Strategies for Meetings and Presentations

Meetings and presentations, two cornerstones of workplace communication, can be particularly challenging for introverts. Often, the expectation is for rapid-fire exchanges, boisterous brainstorming, and confident projection. But true effectiveness lies in clarity, conciseness, and impact. Embrace these strategies to make your communication resonate in the workplace:

- Embrace Preparation: Introverts thrive on thoughtful planning. Invest time in understanding the meeting agenda, anticipating potential questions, and crafting concise talking points. This preparedness empowers you to speak with confidence and clarity when your turn arrives.

- Strategic Intervention: While others might fill the air with words, introverts possess the superpower of attentive listening. Absorb the conversation, identify key points, and consider how your unique perspective can add value. Intervene strategically, offering well-thought-out insights or insightful questions that move the discussion forward. Remember, quality contributions, not quantity, leave a lasting impression.

- The Power of Direct Communication: One-on-one interactions are often more comfortable for introverts. Utilize this strength to schedule meetings with key colleagues or decision-makers before or after large gatherings. In focused discussions, your thoughtful analysis and nuanced observations can shine, influencing decisions in a powerful way.

Building Bridges: One Connection at a Time
Building strong relationships is crucial for professional success, and introverts have the potential to forge deep and meaningful connections. Move beyond the extroverted ideal of large social circles and focus on quality over quantity. Cultivate your introverted strength of genuine interest and active listening to build trusted relationships that benefit you and your career.

Introverts crave authenticity and depth. Instead of scattering your energy on fleeting interactions, actively seek out colleagues who share your values and interests. Engage in thoughtful conversations, offer genuine support, and be a reliable confidante. These bonds, built on shared understanding and mutual respect, will become your strongest professional anchors.

Forget crowded networking events. Leverage your introverted preference for smaller gatherings by initiating one-on-one lunches, coffee breaks, or casual after-work conversations. These focused interactions allow you to build genuine connections and establish professional relationships that are far more valuable than fleeting exchanges in loud rooms.

Your introspective nature and sharp analytical skills can make you a valuable source of wisdom and advice. Offer thoughtful feedback, provide insightful solutions, and be a reliable advocate for others. This quiet leadership earns trust and respect, paving the way for strong professional relationships and career advancement.

Leveraging Introverted Strengths: From Quiet Power to Enduring Success

The workplace often underestimates the power of introverted qualities. Yet, within your preference for solitude, your deep analytical mind, and your thoughtful observations lie potent tools for success. Embrace these unique strengths and see how they can propel you forward:

While others juggle multiple tasks and engage in superficial interactions, your focused attention becomes a valuable asset. Pay close attention to details, absorb information deeply, and analyze situations with a critical eye. This meticulous approach often leads to innovative solutions and insightful decisions that others might miss.

Introverts naturally take time for introspection, processing information and formulating responses before rushing into action. This reflective capacity allows you to make well-considered decisions, strategize effectively, and anticipate potential challenges. In a fast-paced world, your thoughtful approach can offer invaluable stability and wisdom.

In a world dominated by loud voices, introverts can sometimes hesitate to share their thoughts. However, when you do speak, your carefully considered contributions carry weight. Express your ideas with clarity and confidence, focusing on quality over quantity. Your thoughtful insights can spark productive discussions, solve complex problems, and influence decisions in impactful ways.

Your success path is not paved with the same boisterous noise as that of your extroverted colleagues. Your path is one of quiet confidence, thoughtful reflection, and insightful contributions. Embrace your unique strengths, navigate the workplace on your own terms, and watch as your introverted power propels you towards accomplishments that resonate. Let the world discover that success whispers just as loudly as it shouts, and that introverts are not merely participants, but architects of their own triumphant life.

8.3 Networking Strategies Without Draining Energy

For many introverts, the word "networking" conjures images of crowded rooms, forced small talk, and the exhausting pretense of being someone you're not. In a world that often glorifies the extrovert ideal, the pressure to "put yourself out there" can feel like an overwhelming burden. But here's the secret: introverts can not only network effectively, but they can do so in a way that aligns with their strengths and replenishes their energy, not depletes it.

Embrace the Power of Online Platforms

The internet is an introvert's networking haven. Forget the awkward silences and forced introductions. Online platforms allow you to connect with like-minded individuals at your own pace, from the comfort of your own space.

Join online groups and forums dedicated to your industry or interests. These platforms offer a wealth of information, resources, and opportunities to connect with peers and mentors. Participate in discussions, share your knowledge, and build your online presence. Remember, introverts excel at deep listening and thoughtful communication, which can shine through in written interactions.

Utilize platforms like LinkedIn and Twitter strategically. Follow thought leaders and influencers in your field, engage in relevant conversations, and showcase your expertise through posts and articles. Building an online network allows you to connect with potential collaborators, clients, or employers without the pressure of face-to-face interaction.

Also attend online conferences, workshops, and webinars related to your field. These events offer valuable learning opportunities and the chance to connect with others remotely. Take advantage of Q&A sessions and chat features to interact with speakers and participants on your own terms. Remember, introverts often excel at absorbing information and formulating thoughtful questions, making virtual events an ideal platform to contribute insights and build connections.

Attend Targeted Events for Meaningful Connections
While large, generic networking events might feel overwhelming, strategically choosing smaller, focused gatherings can be a rewarding experience for introverts. Look for events related to your specific industry, niche interests, or professional goals. These events tend to attract a more targeted audience, increasing the likelihood of meeting individuals with whom you share genuine connections.

- Go beyond the name tags: Don't just collect business cards and engage in superficial small talk. Approach networking events with a genuine interest in connecting with people. Actively listen to others, ask insightful questions, and focus on finding common ground. Remember, the goal is to build relationships, not just collect contacts.

- Plan your interactions: Don't try to conquer the entire event in one go. Pace yourself, choose a few individuals you'd like to connect with, and dedicate your energy to engaging in meaningful conversations with them. It's better to have a few deep connections than a handful of superficial ones.

- Leave when you need to: Introverts have a limited social energy reserve. Don't push yourself to the point of exhaustion. If you're feeling drained, politely excuse yourself and take a break. Remember, it's okay to prioritize your well-being and recharge for future interactions.

Unveiling Introverted Networking Gems

With your introverted superpowers identified, let's explore alternative networking methods that cater to your preferences:

- Online Networking Platforms: Embrace the digital world! Leverage platforms like LinkedIn, Twitter, or industry-specific forums to connect with professionals in your field. Participate in online discussions, share your expertise, and contribute to relevant groups. Engaging in meaningful online interactions opens doors to potential collaborations, mentorships, and even job opportunities. Remember, online networking allows you to connect at your own pace and engage in thoughtful conversations without the energy drain of traditional networking events.

- One-on-one Coffee Chats: Ditch the crowded spaces and opt for personalized coffee meetings. Reach out to individuals you admire or find interesting within your network, and propose a casual one-on-one coffee chat. This personalized approach allows for deeper conversations, genuine connection, and valuable career advice. Remember, introverts often excel in one-on-one interactions, so tailor your networking experience to your strengths.

- Niche Events and Workshops: Skip the generic conferences and seek out smaller, specialized events or workshops aligned with your interests. These focused gatherings offer a more intimate setting, making it easier to connect with like-minded individuals and potential collaborators. You'll find yourself surrounded by others passionate about your niche, allowing for engaging discussions and meaningful connections.

- Volunteering and Professional Organizations: Giving back to the community is a fantastic way to meet like-minded individuals while building your skills and network. Find volunteer opportunities or organizations related to your field. Contributing your time and expertise while interacting with professionals fosters camaraderie and valuable connections. Remember, introverts often flourish in meaningful pursuits, and volunteering can be a rewarding way to network while making a positive impact.

- Build Your Digital Brand: In today's digital age, your online presence matters. Start a blog, share your expertise on social media, or contribute to online publications. Establishing yourself as a thought leader in your field attracts potential collaborators, clients, and mentors. Remember, online visibility doesn't require constant self-promotion. Focus on high-quality content and insightful contributions, and your personal brand will organically draw like-minded individuals to your network.

Practicing Active Listening and Fostering Genuine Connections

True networking isn't about self-promotion; it's about building genuine connections. As introverts, our natural strength lies in active listening and thoughtful communication. These skills are invaluable in building trust and establishing lasting relationships.

Pay close attention to what others are saying, ask clarifying questions, and show genuine interest in their experiences and perspectives. This not only makes you a more engaging conversationalist but also allows you to build rapport and create a sense of trust.

You shouldn't aim to collect as many connections as possible. Instead, prioritize quality interactions with individuals who share your values and interests. These connections will be more meaningful and mutually beneficial in the long run.

And more importantly, don't try to be someone you're not. Introverts often possess unique perspectives and insights that can be valuable to others. Embrace your introverted nature and let your authentic personality shine through. People connect with those who are genuine and relatable.

Follow up and nurture relationships with guest in after party. Building connections doesn't stop after the initial interaction. Follow up with the individuals you met, send a thoughtful email, or connect on LinkedIn. Show them you're genuinely interested in staying in touch and developing the relationship further.

Remember, introverts are not social recluses. We crave meaningful connections, just on our own terms. You can build a strong network that supports your career aspirations without compromising your introverted nature. Embrace your quiet strength, focus on quality over quantity, and watch your success blossom, one meaningful connection at a time.

Chapter 9: Negotiation and Leadership

9.1 Understanding Introverted Leadership Styles

For centuries, extroversion has been synonymous with leadership. Images of charismatic figures commanding rooms with booming voices and magnetic personalities fill our collective imagination. But what if introverted leaders, with their inherent strengths and nuanced approaches, represent a potent, yet underutilized force in the leadership landscape?

Unveiling the Introverted Leader's Strengths

Introverts often possess a potent arsenal of hidden leadership qualities. We are gifted listeners, absorbing information meticulously before formulating thoughtful responses. This attentiveness enables us to truly hear our team members, understand their concerns, and foster a culture of open communication. Introverts tend to be analytical and strategic thinkers. We weigh decisions carefully, considering all angles before charting a course of action. This measured approach minimizes impulsive decisions and fosters well-considered strategies that benefit the collective good.

Our inherent preference for solitude translates into valuable introspective time. We utilize moments of quiet to reflect on experiences, analyze situations, and formulate innovative solutions. This introspective ability also fuels self-awareness, allowing us to recognize our strengths and limitations, leading to effective delegation and empowered teams. Furthermore, introverts often possess a knack for building deep and meaningful relationships. We invest time and energy in understanding individuals, earning their trust and loyalty through genuine connection. This fosters a collaborative environment where team members feel valued and motivated to contribute their best.

Harmonizing Introversion with Effective Leadership

While introverted qualities contribute immensely to leadership, harmonizing them with effective leadership practices is crucial. Introverts must embrace their strengths without diminishing their visibility or impact. Here's how:

1. Lead by Example: While public speaking may not be your forte, you can lead by setting ethical standards, upholding values, and demonstrating dedication through your actions. Your team will appreciate your consistent presence and unwavering commitment, even if it manifests differently than the "larger-than-life" leader stereotype.

2. Empower Your Team: Introverts often excel at delegation, trusting their team members to excel in areas where they shine. Delegate tasks effectively, provide clear instructions and support, and celebrate individual achievements. This empowers your team, builds trust, and allows you to focus on your strategic strengths.

3. Harness the Power of Asynchronous Communication: Introverts tend to thrive in environments that allow for thoughtful communication. Leverage email, messaging

platforms, and project management tools to communicate effectively on your own terms. This allows you to carefully formulate your thoughts, express yourself clearly, and avoid the draining aspects of constant meetings and impromptu discussions.

4. Embrace Collaboration: While solitude fuels your introverted spirit, remember that leadership thrives on collaboration. Schedule regular one-on-one meetings with team members, build a strong support network, and actively seek diverse perspectives. By fostering open communication and collaborative problem-solving, you tap into the collective intelligence of your team, enriching your leadership path.

Navigating Team Dynamics and Decision-Making

Leading can be challenging, especially for introverts navigating team dynamics and decision-making processes. Here are some tips:

1. Build Trust and Psychological Safety: Introverts thrive in environments where they feel safe to voice their opinions without judgment. Foster a culture of psychological safety where open communication and respectful disagreement are encouraged. This allows your team members to contribute freely, regardless of their personality type.

2. Facilitate Constructive Discussions: Introverts prefer focused, meaningful conversations over large, boisterous group discussions. Create opportunities for smaller, focused discussions where everyone has a chance to contribute.

You can utilize techniques like round-robin sharing or anonymous feedback to ensure all voices are heard.

3. Seek Diverse Perspectives: While your analytical mind offers valuable insights, ensure you consider diverse perspectives before making decisions. Utilize your team's strengths, delegate tasks that leverage specific expertise, and actively seek feedback from your team members. This holistic approach leads to well-rounded decisions that benefit the entire group.

4. Lead with Confidence: Remember, your introverted qualities do not diminish your leadership capabilities. Believe in your strengths, communicate your vision with clarity, and make decisions with conviction. Your quiet confidence will inspire your team and pave the way for successful leadership.

Introverted leadership is not a lesser version of extroverted leadership; it's a different, yet equally effective path to success. By leveraging your inherent strengths, harmonizing your tendencies with effective leadership practices, and navigating team dynamics with finesse, you can forge a unique and impactful leadership style that inspires, empowers, and achieves remarkable results. Embrace your introverted nature, lead from your quiet power within, and rewrite the narrative of what it means to be a successful leader in today's world.

9.2 Tips for Effective Negotiation for Introvert

The world of negotiation and leadership often conjures images of charismatic extroverts, commanding attention and closing deals with booming voices and unwavering confidence. But what if you're an introvert, someone who thrives on quiet contemplation and nuanced communication? Does that mean success in these arenas is out of reach? Absolutely not. In fact, introverts possess a unique set of strengths that can make them formidable negotiators and effective leaders, once they learn to harness their power and navigate the extroverted landscape. Negotiation is a crucial skill in every walk of life, impacting everything from salary discussions to project proposals to navigating personal relationships.

Leveraging Introverted Strengths to Success in Negotiation

1. Deep Listening and Observation: Introverts possess the invaluable skill of active listening. We pay close attention to verbal and nonverbal cues, absorbing information not just through words but also through tone, body language, and subtle shifts in mood. This ability makes us exceptional at understanding the other party's needs and motivations, a key advantage in any negotiation. Imagine a chess player meticulously studying their opponent's moves – introverts bring that same analytical focus to understanding the bargaining landscape.

2. Preparation and Strategic Planning: Introverts thrive on careful planning and thoughtful analysis. Before entering a

negotiation, we can research the topic, anticipate potential arguments, and formulate clear objectives. This meticulous preparation ensures we approach the table with confidence and clarity, knowing exactly what we want and how to achieve it. Think of it like building a sturdy bridge to your desired outcome – introverts lay the groundwork for a smooth and successful crossing.

3. Calm and Composed Demeanor: The emotional intensity of traditional negotiation can be overwhelming for many introverts. However, our inherent calmness and composure serve us well in these situations. We are less prone to impulsive reactions or getting swept away by heated exchanges, allowing us to maintain a level head and think strategically throughout the negotiation. Picture a steady sailboat weathering a storm – introverts maintain their course amidst the inevitable turbulence of negotiation.

4. Collaborative Problem-Solving: Introverts often excel at collaborative problem-solving. We value open communication, active listening, and finding mutually beneficial solutions. This empathetic approach allows us to build rapport with the other party, understand their concerns, and work together to reach a win-win outcome. Think of it like weaving a tapestry of shared interests – introverts can create solutions that benefit everyone involved.

Balancing Assertiveness with Introverted Tendencies

While embracing your introverted strengths is crucial, finding the right balance between assertiveness and your natural reserve is equally important. Here are some tips:

- Prepare assertive phrases: Formulate clear and concise sentences that communicate your needs and objectives. Practice saying things like "I want..." or "My proposal is..." with confidence. Remember, assertiveness does not equal aggression; it simply means stating your desires clearly and directly.

- Focus on facts and logic: Present your arguments based on data, research, and objective evidence. This approach leverages your introverted strengths of analysis and preparation, grounding the conversation in facts and removing room for emotional manipulation.

- Don't be afraid to take breaks: Introverts often need time to recharge and process information. If the negotiation feels draining, politely excuse yourself for a short break to gather your thoughts and composure. Remember, taking a calculated pause can strengthen your resolve and sharpen your focus.

- Utilize alternative communication methods: If face-to-face negotiation feels overwhelming, consider proposing email communication or utilizing collaborative tools like online documents. This allows you to communicate effectively while minimizing direct social interaction.

Developing a Negotiation Style Aligned with Personal Values

Ultimately, your negotiation style should reflect your personal values and goals. Introverts are not a monolith; some may prefer a direct and concise approach, while others may favor a more collaborative and relationship-based strategy. The key is to find a method that feels authentic and comfortable for you while also achieving your desired outcomes.

1. The collaborative negotiator: For introverts who value harmony and win-win outcomes, the collaborative approach is ideal. Focus on understanding your opponent's needs, building rapport, and finding solutions that benefit both parties.

2. The data-driven negotiator: Introverts who excel at analysis can leverage their strength by using facts, figures, and evidence to support their arguments. Present your data clearly and concisely, leaving no room for speculation or misinterpretation.

3. The silent negotiator: Some introverts prefer to communicate primarily through written proposals and documents. This approach can be effective, especially when dealing with individuals who favor a faster, more streamlined negotiation process.

Ultimately, the best negotiation style is one that feels authentic and comfortable for you. Don't be afraid to experiment and find what works best for your personality and the specific situation at hand. Your introversion is not a weakness in negotiation; it's a unique set of strengths that can be used to your advantage to success in any negotiation.

9.3 Strategies for Introverted Leaders

In a world that often trumpets the virtues of extroverted charisma and boundless energy, introverted leaders can sometimes feel like shadows on the wall, their quiet strength underestimated. But step aside, misconceptions! The truth is, introverted leadership offers a unique blend of strengths that can forge powerful teams, navigate complex negotiations, and foster environments where everyone thrives. While the introverted leader may not dominate the room with booming pronouncements or bask in the constant buzz of social interaction, their unique strengths offer a nuanced and well-considered decisions as quality leadership.

Building a Leadership Style Rooted in Introversion

Introverted leaders don't need to contort themselves into extroverted molds to succeed. Instead, they leverage their inherent strengths to build a leadership style that empowers both themselves and their teams. This begins with self-awareness. Recognizing the need for solitude to recharge, the power of reflective thinking, and the preference for focused one-on-one interactions allows introverted leaders to design workflows and communication strategies that align with their natural tendencies.

Imagine a sculptor, not wielding a hammer but a chisel. Each deliberate stroke reveals the form, each quiet moment spent in contemplation shapes the masterpiece. Introverted leaders work similarly. They carve out time for deep analysis, listen intently to diverse perspectives, and meticulously craft solutions, all while prioritizing their own well-being to maintain their creative and strategic edge.

This self-awareness also fosters authenticity. Introverted leaders don't need to force boisterous pronouncements or pretend to thrive in constant social whirlwinds. They embrace their quiet confidence, their thoughtful demeanor, and their preference for meaningful interactions. This authenticity fosters trust and respect, as team members recognize their leader's genuine nature and appreciate the depth of their insights.

Cultivating a Positive Work Environment Through Introverted Leadership

Introverted leaders, with their natural focus on collaboration and building trust, excel at creating positive work environments. They prioritize active listening, creating safe spaces where team members feel comfortable sharing ideas without fear of judgment or interruption. This fosters a culture of open communication, where diverse perspectives are valued and disagreements are addressed constructively, leading to better-informed decisions and a stronger sense of team cohesion.

Imagine a serene garden, not a cacophony of blooms but a harmonious blend of vibrant colors and delicate textures.

Introverted leaders cultivate such environments, providing their team with the space and support to blossom. They delegate effectively, recognizing individual strengths and empowering team members to take ownership of their work. This fosters a sense of trust and responsibility, leading to a more engaged and productive workforce.

Introverted leaders also understand the importance of boundaries. They recognize their need for solitude and downtime, and they prioritize creating a culture that respects these boundaries. This might involve setting clear expectations around email responsiveness, scheduling regular "quiet hours," and encouraging team members to communicate asynchronously whenever possible. By prioritizing their own well-being and respecting the needs of others, introverted leaders create a sustainable and healthy work environment for everyone.

Navigating Challenges Unique to Introverted Leaders

Despite their strengths, introverted leaders also face unique challenges. Overcoming the societal biases that often equate leadership with extroversion is one such hurdle. Introverted leaders may need to actively advocate for their leadership style, reminding others that quiet confidence, thoughtful analysis, and deep listening are valuable assets in any leadership position.

Additionally, introverted leaders may struggle with situations that demand quick action or constant visibility. Navigating these situations effectively requires preparation and strategic communication. Introverted leaders can delegate tasks that require high-energy interaction, leverage technology to communicate effectively with large groups, and ensure they have sufficient time for reflection before making important decisions.

Finally, introverted leaders may need to step outside their comfort zones at times. Public speaking, networking events, and other social interactions can be draining, but they can also be valuable opportunities to connect with stakeholders and build influence. Introverted leaders can approach these situations with planning and preparation, focusing on connecting with individuals and engaging in meaningful conversations rather than trying to be the life of the party.

The world of leadership needs introverts. Their quiet strength, thoughtful approach, and focus on collaboration offer a valuable counterpoint to the extroverted ideal. By embracing their unique strengths and navigating their challenges, introverted leaders can create positive work environments, foster innovation, and achieve remarkable success. Remember, the quietest gardens often bloom the most vibrant flowers, and the most impactful leaders are not always the loudest voices in the room. So, introverted leaders, stand tall, embrace your strengths, and lead with quiet confidence, knowing that your unique voice has the power to shape the world around you.

Chapter 10: Personal Branding

10.1 Building a Personal Brand Aligned with Authenticity

In the bustling world of personal branding, a siren buzz often beckons: reinvent yourself, tailor your image to fit the mold, and project a persona that screams "extrovert in disguise." But for introverts, this words can feel jarring, a discordant note in the harmony of their authentic selves. Yet, building a personal brand doesn't necessitate sacrificing your introverted essence; it's about crafting a narrative that amplifies your unique strengths, resonates with your values, and illuminates your brilliance, even in the quietest corners. How do we build a brand that resonates with the world while remaining true to our introspective nature? The answer lies not in mimicking extroverted archetypes, but in leveraging the very essence of our introversion – our depth, our focus, and our quiet power – to craft a brand that shines with authenticity.

Defining Your Authentic Self

Personal branding begins with a profound excavation – unearthing the core of your being. This isn't a quest for external validation, but a path of introspective exploration. Ask yourself: what ignites your curiosity? What fuels your passion? What values guide your actions and decisions? Are you a meticulous researcher, a skilled storyteller, a creative problem solver, or a compassionate listener? Delve into these depths, not to sculpt a persona, but to discover the essence that makes you, you.

Introverts often possess a hidden treasure trove of introspective wisdom. We are the silent observers, the keen listeners, the deep thinkers who process information with nuanced understanding. We value meaningful connections over fleeting acquaintances, and our quiet energy can be the wellspring of insightful ideas and creative solutions. Embrace these qualities, not as liabilities, but as the cornerstones of your authentic brand.

Personal branding is not just about what you do, it's about who you are. As introverts, it's crucial to ensure that the image we project aligns with our core values. Do you value authenticity and sincerity? Then let your brand reflect your genuine personality, not a fabricated persona. Do you champion thoughtful action over impulsive noise? Then let your brand showcase your deep work and insightful contributions, not a constant barrage of social media updates.

Leveraging Introverted Qualities for a Unique Personal Brand

Now, let's translate your introverted strengths into a captivating brand narrative. Instead of forcing yourself into the extroverted mold, turn your introspective nature into a beacon of depth and thoughtfulness. Share your insights through well-crafted writing, insightful podcasts, or captivating online courses. Your quiet confidence can become a powerful asset, conveying expertise and trustworthiness.

Introverts often possess a natural gift for storytelling. We are the observers, the listeners, the ones who glean meaning from the subtlest details. Use this storytelling power to craft your personal brand narrative. Share your story of self-discovery, your unique perspective on the world, and the passions that ignite your introverted soul. Let your story resonate with others who may be navigating the same path, seeking guidance and understanding in a world that often overlooks the power of quiet introspection.

Additionally, introverts are masters of the slow burn. We don't need the constant spotlight to shine. Cultivate a personal brand that thrives on quality over quantity. Build a loyal following through genuine interactions, thoughtful content, and a commitment to creating value. Your introverted nature allows you to connect on a deeper level, fostering meaningful relationships that transcend the superficiality of the online world.

Aligning Values with Your Personal Brand Image
Personal branding is not just about your outward image; it's about aligning your projected persona with your core values. As an introvert, you may value authenticity, integrity, and thoughtful communication. Let these values be the guiding compass of your brand narrative. Create content that reflects your genuine beliefs, engage in conversations that align with your principles, and collaborate with individuals who share your values.

Remember, authenticity is not about perfection; it's about embracing your genuine self, flaws and all. Don't shy away from expressing your introverted perspective, even if it challenges the extroverted norm. Your unique voice and perspective are what make your brand stand out, attracting those who resonate with your authentic self.

Building a personal brand as an introvert is not about dimming your light; it's about illuminating your unique brilliance. It's about crafting a narrative that whispers wisdom, sparks curiosity, and fosters meaningful connections. It's about showcasing your introverted strengths, not in spite of your introversion, but because of it.

So, embrace your introspective nature, let your values guide your brand narrative, and unleash the power of your authentic self. It's about finding your voice and using it to connect with those who truly matter. So, introverts, let your quiet glow illuminate the world. Let your introspective wisdom guide the way. And let your authentic self be the foundation of a brand that is not just successful, but meaningful, impactful, and uniquely your own.

10.2 Utilizing Online Platforms for Self-Promotion

The very thought of self-promotion, of blasting your achievements across the digital landscape, might send shivers down an introvert's spine. For those who recharge in quiet corners and find solace in thoughtful conversations, the extroverted world of online self-branding can feel like a cacophony of forced interactions and relentless self-promotion. But here's the truth: building an online presence isn't just for extroverts. It's a powerful tool for anyone, including introverts, to showcase their skills, connect with like-minded individuals, and forge professional paths aligned with their authentic selves.

The key lies in strategically navigating the digital world, choosing platforms and approaches that resonate with your introverted strengths. Ditch the pressure to conform to extroverted ideals of constant updates and public validation. Instead, craft an online presence that reflects your unique voice, respects your need for downtime, and cultivates meaningful connections rather than chasing empty popularity.

Selecting the Right Stage

Not all online platforms are created equal. While some thrive on fast-paced exchanges and fleeting trends, others cater to thoughtful dialogue and in-depth engagement. Before jumping in, consider platforms that align with your introverted communication style:

- LinkedIn: This professional networking site allows you to build a digital resume, highlight your skills and experience, and connect with individuals in your field through targeted groups and discussions. Introverts can leverage LinkedIn's structured and professional environment to strategically build their network without the pressure of endless social interactions.

- Medium: This blogging platform caters to longer-form writing, allowing introverts to delve into their expertise and share their unique perspectives without the constraints of character limits. You can choose topics that truly resonate with you, build a community of engaged readers, and establish yourself as a thought leader in your field, all at your own pace.

- Podcasts: The introverted listener might surprise themselves by enjoying the intimacy and depth of podcast conversations. But introverts can also take the mic and launch their own shows, exploring topics they're passionate about and attracting listeners who share their interests. Podcasts offer a platform for introverts to express themselves on their own terms, connecting with their audience through thoughtful discussions rather than bombastic performances.

- Niche Social Media Communities: Introverts often find solace in smaller, more focused online communities dedicated to specific interests or industries. These communities offer a safe space to engage in meaningful discussions, share knowledge, and build genuine connections with people who understand your passions. Look for groups aligned with your interests and expertise, and participate thoughtfully, contributing your unique insights and voice.

Building an Introverted Brand

Once you've chosen your platform, it's time to craft an online persona that reflects your authentic self. Here are some tips for introverts to build a presence that showcases their strengths:

- Focus on quality over quantity: Don't overwhelm yourself with the pressure to constantly post. Instead, prioritize quality content that showcases your expertise and offers genuine value to your audience. Write insightful articles, engage in thoughtful discussions, and share content that reflects your unique perspective.

- Embrace long-form communication: Introverts often excel at expressing themselves in detail. Utilize platforms like Medium or your own blog to share in-depth analyses, insightful essays, or detailed project descriptions. This allows you to delve into your expertise and connect with readers who appreciate well-crafted thought pieces.

- Prioritize meaningful connections: Don't chase followers or popularity. Instead, focus on building genuine connections with individuals who share your interests and values. Engage in thoughtful conversations, respond to comments with meaningful replies, and actively participate in online communities.

- Curate your content: Be selective about what you share online. Not every aspect of your life needs to be public. Maintain a healthy balance between personal and professional, sharing insightful pieces of your expertise while safeguarding your privacy and ensuring your online presence reflects the professional image you wish to cultivate.

Navigating the Personal-Professional Balancing Act

Introverts often excel in deep, one-on-one interactions. But the online world can feel impersonal and overwhelming. Here are some tips for navigating the balance between personal and professional online presence:

- Set clear boundaries: Decide what level of personal information you're comfortable sharing online. You don't have to reveal everything about yourself to build a successful personal brand. Set boundaries and stick to them, protecting your privacy while still sharing enough to connect with your audience.

- Create separate channels: If you enjoy sharing personal updates but want to maintain a professional image, consider creating separate accounts for personal and professional purposes. This allows you to express yourself on your own terms while keeping your professional brand focused and polished.

- Utilize privacy settings: Most platforms offer various privacy settings. Take advantage of these tools to control who sees your content and who can interact with you. This way, you can create a safe and comfortable online environment and greater control over your online presence and protects your privacy.

The key of self promotion is to choose platforms where you can express yourself authentically without feeling drained or overwhelmed while carefully balancing personal and professional area. Don't feel pressured to be everywhere at once. Focus on building a strong presence on one or two platforms that resonate with your introverted nature. And look at your steadily growth over time.

10.3 Strategies for Long-Term Brand Building

Building a personal brand isn't a one-and-done sprint; it's a meticulously crafted marathon. Imagine meticulously carving a statue, refining each stroke with precision, constantly shaping and reshaping to reveal the masterpiece within. Just as the sculptor's vision endures through countless chisel marks, your personal brand thrives on consistent reinforcement and thoughtful evolution.

1. The Echo Chamber of Consistent Reinforcement

The first crucial ingredient for long-term brand building is consistency. Think of it as the steady stream of logs feeding the fire. Showcasing your expertise consistently, whether through blog posts, online communities, or carefully curated social media presence, helps etch your unique value proposition in the minds of others. This consistency, however, doesn't require constant extroverted bursts. Introverts thrive on focused bursts of energy, so schedule your brand-building activities in ways that work for you. A few insightful articles published strategically throughout the week can have a more impactful and sustainable effect than daily, fleeting interactions.

In practice, consistency translates to various dimensions. Maintain a coherent style and tone across your online platforms, be it writing, videos, or podcasts. Let your values and expertise shine through consistently, guiding the content you choose to engage with and share. This doesn't mean becoming a monotonous record player; it's about creating a core brand narrative with room for exploration and growth within its framework.

Consistency isn't a rigid cage, but a fertile ground for your brand to flourish. As you experiment with new formats or delve deeper into your niche, ensure these explorations align with your core message and values. The audience connects with the familiar, but they're also enticed by thoughtful evolution. Keep the melody consistent, but introduce new instruments to enrich the experience.

2. The Feedback Loop

Building a brand isn't about constructing a towering monument and declaring it impervious to feedback. True growth, like a majestic redwood, requires flexibility and adaptation. Embrace constructive criticism as the gentle breeze whispering through your branches, guiding you towards greater resilience and refinement.

Seek feedback from mentors, colleagues, and peers. Don't shy away from constructive criticism, even if it stings initially. Remember, a temporary discomfort can pave the way for long-term improvement. Analyze feedback thoughtfully, separating personal attacks from genuine insights. If a recurring theme emerges, it's likely a blind spot worth exploring.

Adapting your brand based on feedback doesn't mean betraying your core values. It's about refining your message, honing your skills, and ensuring your brand resonates with its intended audience. Think of it as adjusting the sails of your ship, not changing its destination. You may need to navigate different currents, but your life's true purpose remains unwavering.

3. Building Your Brand Support System

No sculptor works in isolation, and neither should you when building your personal brand. Seek out a network of individuals who champion your values, amplify your message, and provide unwavering support. These are your brand ambassadors, the cheerleaders who echo your melody and strengthen its reach.

Actively cultivate relationships with like-minded individuals within your industry or niche. Collaborate on projects, guest on each other's podcasts or blogs, and participate in joint webinars or workshops. This cross-pollination of ideas and audiences not only benefits your individual brands but also creates a vibrant ecosystem where everyone thrives.

Don't neglect the power of online communities. Engage in relevant forums, contribute meaningfully to discussions, and connect with individuals who share your passions. These digital connections can blossom into invaluable collaborations and offer a platform to showcase your expertise and build trust with a wider audience.

Remember, your network is not a one-way street. Be an active supporter of others, offer your expertise and encouragement, and celebrate their successes. This genuine sense of community fosters loyalty and amplifies the collective brand message far beyond individual voices.

Building a personal brand is not an endeavor with a finish line; it's a lifelong story of discovery, adaptation, and growth. Consistency is the foundation, feedback is the guiding breeze, and your network is the amplifying wind. Embrace these elements, refine your brand with each step, and watch your authentic voice resonate with the world, leaving an indelible mark that transcends fleeting trends.

Chapter 11: Personal Relationship Success for Introverts

11.1 Finding the Right Partner

For introverts, navigating the often-turbulent waters of romantic relationships can feel like steering a sailboat through a storm. Our preference for solitude, measured communication, and deep introspection can seem at odds with the outward displays of affection, constant chatter, and social whirlwinds often associated with romance. But fear not, fellow introverts! Finding a partner who understands and cherishes your unique nature is not only possible, it can blossom into a relationship of profound intimacy and unwavering support.

Seeking a Partner Who Understands and Values Introverted Needs

The search for the "right" partner begins with an honest self-examination. Understand your introverted needs, the way your energy ebbs and flows, and the environments that replenish your reserves. Do you thrive on deep, meaningful conversations fueled by shared passions, or do quiet evenings spent reading side-by-side suffice? Do you need regular solo retreats to recharge, or can you maintain your introverted core within a bustling social life?

Once you have a map of your own emotional landscape, don't shy away from communicating your needs openly and honestly. Don't apologize for your introverted nature, but present it as the valuable facet it is. Seek individuals who appreciate the thoughtful silences that punctuate your conversations, who find comfort in shared contemplation, and who understand that your quiet intensity does not equate to disinterest.

Remember, your partner needn't be another introvert (though a fellow introspective soul can certainly create a harmonious haven). Look for individuals who possess qualities that complement your introverted nature. Someone who is a patient listener, who values thoughtful gestures over grand displays, and who finds genuine joy in the quiet intimacies of shared interests and passions.

Speaking of passions, shared hobbies and interests can be the bridge that connects your introverted world to another's. Engaging in activities you both enjoy, whether it's exploring obscure art galleries, delving into philosophical discussions, or losing yourselves in the pages of a shared book, fosters a deeper connection that transcends the need for constant social interaction. Remember, introverts often build connections through shared experiences and intellectual exchange, creating a strong foundation for a lasting and mutually fulfilling relationship.

Introverts naturally gravitate towards smaller, more meaningful social circles. Don't feel pressured to conform to societal expectations of large friend groups and constant socializing. Celebrate your partner's close connections, and nurture your own intimate bonds. Remember, the quality of your relationships is far more valuable than the quantity. A handful of genuine friends who understand and support you can provide a deeper sense of belonging and fulfillment than a room full of acquaintances.

Understanding and appreciating your own introverted strengths is crucial in attracting a compatible partner. Introverts are often gifted with exceptional listening skills, deep empathy, and insightful observations. They bring a sense of calm and stability to relationships, and their thoughtful approach to problem-solving can be invaluable. Remind yourself that your introversion is not a weakness, but a unique set of strengths that can enrich any relationship.

Tips for Introverts Seeking the Right Partner

- Seek authentic connections over fleeting encounters: Prioritize quality over quantity when it comes to relationships. Focus on building deep, meaningful connections with individuals who resonate with your introverted tendencies and appreciate your thoughtful nature.

- Don't be afraid of online dating: The digital world can be a surprisingly comfortable space for introverts to connect and explore potential partners. Online platforms allow you to present your genuine self without the pressure of immediate face-to-face interaction, giving you time to connect on a deeper level before taking the plunge into the real world.

- Embrace group activities as stepping stones: Participating in activities that align with your hobbies and interests, such as book clubs, hiking groups, or volunteering projects, can help you connect with like-minded individuals in a less pressure-filled environment. Look for individuals who engage genuinely and share your passions, not those who simply seek the spotlight.

- Communicate your needs openly and honestly: Don't expect your partner to automatically understand your introverted needs. Explain to them the way you recharge, the importance of alone time, and your preferred modes of communication. Open and honest communication is crucial for building a relationship where both partners feel respected and understood.

- Don't compromise your core values: While finding common ground is important, you shouldn't have to contort yourself to fit your partner's mold. Stay true to your authentic self and seek someone who appreciates you for who you are, introversion and all.

Finding a partner who understands and values your introverted nature can be a transformative experience. It allows you to be your authentic self, embrace your unique strengths, and experience the joy of a deep and meaningful connection. So, step out there, introverts, with your hearts open and your minds receptive. The world is full of potential partners waiting to discover the depth and beauty that lies within your quiet souls.

11.2 Maintaining Healthy Relationships

In the sun-drenched fields of extroversion, relationships blossom under the constant light of social interaction. But for introverts, love thrives in the quiet gardens of thoughtful connection, nurtured by deliberate attention and carefully-chosen moments of shared experience. Maintaining healthy relationships as an introvert isn't about replicating extroverted norms; it's about cultivating a unique rhythm of love and communication that resonates with your deepest needs.

Scheduling Quality Time

For introverts, energy fluctuates. The vibrant symphony of a crowded party quickly drains our batteries, leaving us needing the restorative silence of solitude. This ebb and flow can be challenging in relationships, particularly when partners have different energy levels.

The solution isn't forcing constant togetherness, but scheduling quality time with intention. Think of it not as a rigid constraint, but as a compass guiding you towards meaningful connection. Instead of marathon social nights, prioritize focused evenings filled with deep conversations, shared activities you both enjoy, or simply sitting in comfortable silence, savoring each other's presence. Remember, quality trumps quantity - a single candlelit dinner can speak volumes compared to a whirlwind weekend that leaves you both depleted.

Introverts often excel at the art of listening. We don't just hear the words; we absorb the emotions, the hesitations, the unspoken subtext. This gift becomes a powerful tool in relationships, allowing us to build bridges of understanding across the gap between individuals.

Active listening, for introverts, isn't just a passive act of receiving information. It's a deliberate balance of engagement, asking thoughtful questions, reflecting back understanding, and creating a safe space for vulnerability. It's about paying attention not just to the words, but to the body language, the silences between words, the subtle nuances that speak volumes. By truly listening, we validate our partners' experiences, weave tapestries of empathy, and foster a connection that transcends mere conversation.

Expressing Love for Introverts

Introverts may not always shout their love from rooftops, but our affection burns deeply, expressed in a nuanced language of quiet gestures and thoughtful actions. Forget the grand pronouncements and public displays; for introverts, love whispers in the gentle touch of a hand, the shared cup of tea in the morning, the meticulously-chosen gift that reflects a cherished memory.

Listen to your partner's love language. Do they cherish words of affirmation? Write them a heartfelt note tucked into their favorite book. Do they thrive on acts of service? Fold their laundry while they're at work, a silent testament to your care. Do they appreciate quality time? Plan a quiet picnic under the stars, just the two of you. Remember, introverted love speaks in gentle rhythms, not booming pronouncements.

Seeking Help When Most Needed

Even the most meticulously kept garden can face challenges. Miscommunication, unmet emotional needs, or unresolved conflicts can become weeds threatening the bloom of your relationship. In such situations, seeking professional help isn't a sign of weakness, but a testament to your commitment to nurturing your love.

Therapists act as master gardeners, helping you identify the weeds, develop tools for communication, and cultivate soil fertile for understanding and growth. Don't shy away from seeking support; remember, sometimes the healthiest gardens are those carefully tended by professionals with experience and expertise.

Remember, your introverted nature is not a barrier to successful relationships, but a unique and valuable lens through which you experience love. Embrace your quiet strength, your deliberate communication, and your heartfelt expressions of affection. By understanding your needs and nurturing your connection with intention, you can cultivate a garden of love that thrives, not despite, but because of your introversion.

This path might not be as loud or ostentatious as the whirlwind romances depicted in movies, but it's no less beautiful. It's a slow waltz of whispered promises, shared sunsets in comfortable silence, and a love that grows strong in the quiet garden of your hearts. In this realm, introverts not only find success, but discover a depth of connection that resonates as powerfully as any grand declaration.

11.3 Building a Support System

For an introvert, navigating the social landscape can feel like traversing a vast, open plain under a blazing sun. While extroverts thrive in the bustling marketplace of human interaction, introverts often yearn for the cool solace of a shaded oasis, a place to recharge and reconnect with their inner selves. Yet, even in this perceived isolation, introverts have an innate need for connection. We crave deep and meaningful relationships, those quiet havens where vulnerabilities can be whispered and laughter shared without fanfare.

Online Communities: Your Digital Shelter

Building a support system for introverts isn't about amassing a vast network of acquaintances; it's about constructing a sturdy shelter, brick by carefully placed brick, filled with individuals who understand the rhythm of our introverted hearts.

The cornerstone of this shelter is often found in connecting with other introverts. In the age of digital connectivity, the internet opens a door to a hidden garden teeming with like-minded souls. Online communities and forums dedicated to introversion provide a refuge where one can shed the pressure to perform and bask in the comfort of shared experiences. Here, conversations flow in gentle streams, punctuated by thoughtful pauses and attentive listening. Introverted humor sparkles in memes and anecdotes, and anxieties melt away in the understanding gazes of digital eyes. These online havens offer a sense of belonging, a comforting reminder that you're not alone in your quietude, that your introverted nature is not a flaw, but a vibrant thread woven into the tapestry of humanity.

However, the bricks and mortar of our support system should not be confined to the virtual realm. Seeking out mentors or coaches who understand the introverted personality can be an invaluable addition. These wise guides, often introverts themselves, offer a beacon of understanding in a world that often seems tailor-made for extroverts. They provide practical strategies for navigating social situations, managing energy levels, and asserting ourselves without compromising our authentic selves. More importantly, they offer validation, a reassuring pat on the back that whispers, "It's okay to be you, to recharge in silence, to find joy in solitude." This validation, this whispered understanding, can be the wind beneath our introverted wings, propelling us to soar in our chosen pursuits.

Prioritizing Self-Care

But let us not forget the foundation upon which all other support rests: prioritizing self-care. For introverts, self-care is not a luxury; it's a necessity. It's the quiet oasis where we replenish our depleted energy reserves, the sanctuary where we nourish our introverted spirit. Self-care for introverts can manifest in countless ways, from losing ourselves in a captivating book to spending a mindful hour in nature's embrace, from savoring a steaming cup of tea in peaceful solitude to indulging in a creative passion that sets our soul ablaze. These seemingly simple acts are not selfish indulgences; they are deliberate investments in our well-being, the fuel that keeps the engine of our introverted story purring smoothly.

Building a support system for introverts is not a one-time event; it's an ongoing process, a balance with the ebb and flow of our social energy. There will be times when online communities offer the perfect solace, while other moments may call for the gentle guidance of a like-minded mentor. And then there will be those blessed intervals where all we need is the sweet embrace of self-care, the nourishment of silence and solitude. The key is to listen to the whispers of our introverted hearts, to understand their unique needs, and to cultivate a support system that reflects this understanding. In doing so, we create a refuge, a haven where our introverted nature can not only survive, but thrive, radiating its quiet strength and unique brilliance into the world.

Remember, dear introvert, your quietude is not a liability; it's a source of power. Your need for solitude is not a weakness; it's a wellspring of creativity and introspection. And your carefully chosen support system is not a crutch; it's a testament to your resilience, a celebration of your introverted spirit. So, build your haven, brick by mindful brick, filled with understanding, acceptance, and the quiet hum of self-care. In this sanctuary, you will discover that success, for introverts, is not about conforming to an extroverted world, but about carving your own path, a path lit by the gentle glow of your authentic introverted self.

Chapter 12: Time Management for Introverts

12.1 Practical Advice on Managing Energy Levels

For introverts, time management isn't just about ticking off to-dos; it's a delicate balance with our precious energy reserves. We thrive on focused effort, thoughtful deliberation, and deep contemplation, but juggling demands and maintaining peak productivity requires an introspective understanding of our unique ebb and flow.

1. Mapping Your Inner Landscape: Recognizing Personal Energy Patterns

Imagine your energy as a fluctuating wellspring, rising and falling throughout the day. As introverts, these fluctuations are often amplified. The morning might offer a surge of focused productivity, while the afternoon may be draped in a veil of introspective quietude. Recognizing these personal patterns is the first step to crafting a schedule that works for you, not against you.

- Track your energy: Keep a simple journal or use a time-tracking app to log your daily activities and emotional states. Notice when you feel most productive, alert, and engaged. Do specific times of day trigger feelings of fatigue or overwhelm? Identifying these peak and dip periods is crucial for optimizing your schedule.

- Honor your natural rhythms: Are you an early bird chirping before dawn or a night owl thriving under the moon? Don't fight your natural inclinations. Schedule demanding tasks for your peak productivity hours and reserve quieter activities for dip periods. Remember, early mornings aren't magically more productive for everyone; embrace your unique chronotype and schedule accordingly.

- Listen to your inner voice: Don't ignore those subtle internal cues. If your mind craves solitude, don't force yourself into a crowded meeting. Conversely, if you're feeling energized and social, take advantage of that window for collaborative tasks. Respecting your introverted needs leads to better time management and avoids unnecessary energy depletion.

2. Building Breaks into Bridges: Incorporating Downtime into Schedules

Unlike their extroverted counterparts, introverts don't recharge in the buzz of constant activity. We need deliberate downtime, quiet sanctuaries where we can replenish our energy and process information. Incorporating these breaks into your schedule isn't a luxury; it's a necessity.

- Schedule your solitude: Don't leave "me-time" to chance. Block out specific times in your calendar dedicated to solitude and introspection. Whether it's a 30-minute afternoon walk, a solo lunch break, or an evening reading session, these intentional breaks become refuges to recharge and revitalize your introverted spirit.

- Embrace "micro-breaks": Short, frequent breaks throughout the day can be lifesavers for introverts. Step away from your screen, take a brisk walk, or simply close your eyes and breathe deeply. These micro-breaks can prevent fatigue from snowballing, refocus your mind, and allow you to return to tasks with renewed energy.

- Create your sanctuary: Designate a space in your home or office that serves as your personal haven. Fill it with elements that soothe your senses: cozy blankets, calming music, inspiring books, or calming plants. This becomes your retreat, a physical manifestation of your need for solitude, where you can unwind and reconnect with yourself.

3. Navigating the Roadblocks: Strategies for Avoiding Burnout and Maintaining Mental Well-being

Even with careful planning, introverts can occasionally hit burnout, a state of chronic exhaustion and emotional overload. Recognizing the warning signs and having clear strategies in place is essential for maintaining your mental well-being and preventing long-term burnout.

- Set boundaries and say no: Introverts often struggle with assertiveness, but saying no is crucial for protecting your energy. Don't overload your schedule with unnecessary commitments. Learn to politely decline requests that drain your reserves and prioritize activities that align with your introverted needs.

- Delegate and collaborate: You don't have to go it alone. Delegate tasks you find draining or outsource responsibilities whenever possible. Collaboration can also be beneficial, but choose your partners wisely. Seek out like-minded individuals who respect your need for solitude and understand the value of focused, introverted work.

- Connect with your support system: Don't underestimate the power of genuine connection. Introverts may crave solitude, but we also need meaningful relationships. Talk to trusted friends, family members, or therapists who understand your introverted nature and offer support without demanding constant social interaction.

- Prioritize self-care: Self-care is not a luxury; it's an essential tool for maintaining your mental well-being. Engage in activities that nourish your spirit, whether it's meditation, nature walks, creative pursuits, or simply spending time with loved ones. Prioritizing self-care ensures you have the emotional and mental reserves to navigate the inevitable challenges of life.

Time management for introverts is not about mimicking extroverted norms; it's about understanding your own rhythm, honoring your needs, and building a life that allows you to flourish. By recognizing your energy patterns, implementing practical strategies, and embracing your unique strengths, you can transform time management from a burden to a tool for success and fulfillment. So, chart your course, introverted explorer, and conquer the ocean of time on your own terms.

12.2 Prioritizing Tasks and Setting Timelines

For introverts, navigating the relentless demands of our time-driven world can feel like swimming against the current. Our need for solitude and focused energy clashes with the constant notifications, overflowing inboxes, and ever-expanding to-do lists. Yet, just as we've learned to thrive in a world built for extroverts, mastering time management can become a powerful tool for introverts, allowing us to channel our unique strengths and work in a way that aligns with our natural rhythms.

Developing Effective Prioritization Techniques

1. The Power of Introverted Analysis: Introverts possess a natural gift for deep thinking and careful analysis. Harness this strength by dedicating time to reflecting on your tasks and identifying those that truly matter. Ask yourself: What aligns with your goals and values? What will have the most significant impact? What tasks, if accomplished, would propel you forward? Use mind maps, lists, or journaling to prioritize based on importance, urgency, and your own introverted preferences. Remember, less is often more for introverts; focusing on a few high-impact tasks can be far more effective than spreading yourself thin across countless less-important ones.

2. The ABCs of Prioritization: Implement a simple yet effective system like the ABC method. Categorize tasks as A (high priority, urgent), B (important, but not urgent), and C (lesser priority, can be delegated or deferred). Focus your energy on A tasks first, dedicating your peak introverted

focus to tackling the most crucial items. Allocate smaller pockets of time for B tasks, and consider outsourcing or delegating C tasks whenever possible. This system ensures you address the most important matters first, without neglecting lesser responsibilities or draining your introverted energy reserves.

3. The Timeboxing Technique: Introverts often thrive on structure and predictability. Utilize the timeboxing technique to segment your day into dedicated blocks for specific tasks. Allocate realistic chunks of time, factoring in your need for breaks and introspective reflection. Sticking to these timeboxes creates a sense of control and prevents tasks from bleeding into your precious personal time. Remember, breaks are not indulgences, but essential recharges for your introverted battery. Utilize these breaks for solo activities like meditation, reading, or simply sitting in quiet contemplation.

Setting Realistic Goals and Timelines
1. Understanding Introverted Timelines: Introverts often operate on different timeframes than extroverts. We may need longer periods of uninterrupted focus to achieve deep work, followed by extended stretches of solitude to recharge. Don't succumb to the pressure of externally imposed deadlines. Acknowledge your introverted tendencies and set realistic goals aligned with your natural rhythm. Break down large projects into smaller, achievable milestones, celebrating each accomplishment along the way. This incremental approach prevents overwhelm and

maintains motivation, reminding you that progress, not perfection, is the true measure of success.

2. Embracing Flexibility: Rigid schedules can be the bane of an introvert's existence. Build flexibility into your timelines, allowing for unforeseen circumstances and your innate need for spontaneous solitude. Leave buffers between tasks, knowing that an unexpected burst of inspiration might require adjustment. Be open to rescheduling meetings or deadlines when necessary, prioritizing your introverted well-being while ensuring responsible fulfillment of your commitments.

3. The Power of "No": Introverts often struggle with saying no due to our desire to be helpful and avoid conflict. However, saying no to unnecessary commitments protects your valuable time and energy. Learn to politely decline tasks that don't align with your priorities or drain your introverted reserves. Remember, saying no to something allows you to say yes to the things that truly matter, both professionally and personally.

Establishing Firm Boundaries for Personal and Professional Life
1. The Sanctuary of Solitude: Introverts need dedicated time and space for solitude to recharge. Establish clear boundaries between your work and personal life, creating a haven for introverted replenishment. This might involve setting specific work hours, utilizing a dedicated workspace, or communicating your need for quiet time to colleagues and family. Respect your own boundaries and

don't be afraid to politely enforce them. Protecting your space for solitude is not selfish, it's essential for your introverted well-being and ultimately, your overall productivity.

2. Minimizing Distractions: The constant barrage of notifications and interruptions can be detrimental to an introvert's focus. Implement strategies to minimize distractions. Silence your phone, close unnecessary browser tabs, and inform colleagues when you need uninterrupted time. Consider utilizing noise-canceling headphones or working in quiet spaces to maximize your introverted focus. Remember, small tweaks to your environment can make a significant difference in your ability to work effectively and recharge peacefully.

3. Communicating Your Introverted Needs: It's okay to openly communicate your introverted needs to colleagues and family, this will release heavy burden and help you to achieve your goals. Explain your most productive hours and when you prefer to disconnect. Explain how solitude helps you recharge and be your most productive self. This provides a clear boundary between the productive phase and recharge phase and allows you to fully relax during your personal hours.

Mastering time management as an introvert is not about forcing yourself to fit into an extroverted phase. It's about understanding your unique needs, respecting your introverted tendencies, and developing strategies that work for you. By prioritizing tasks that align with your values, setting realistic goals and timelines, and establishing firm boundaries, you can create a time management system that

149

fosters productivity, protects your energy, and empowers you to thrive as the introverted individual you are.

12.3 Strategies for Productive Time Use

For introverts, time is a precious resource. While extroverts thrive on the constant buzz of activity, our energy reserves require careful management. Our need for solitude and deliberate energy expenditure clashes with the relentless demands of deadlines, schedules, and the constant buzz of "getting things done." Mastering the art of time management isn't about forcing ourselves into a mold of external pressures, but about crafting a system that honors our introverted needs for solitude, reflection, and focused deep work.

1. Mindfulness as The Introvert's Time Management Secret Weapon

Introverts possess a unique superpower: the ability to step back, observe, and reflect. Harnessing this power through mindfulness can revolutionize your approach to time management. By practicing mindfulness, you cultivate a present-moment awareness, allowing you to consciously choose where to direct your energy and attention. This intentional approach is key for introverts, as it prevents us from getting swept away by external demands and ensures we prioritize tasks that align with our values and goals.

Here are some practical ways to incorporate mindfulness into your time management:

- Meditation: Start your day with a few minutes of meditation, focusing on your breath and quieting your inner chatter. This sets the tone for a mindful day, allowing you to approach tasks with clear intention.

- Time Audits: Regularly conduct time audits, tracking where your energy and attention are going. This awareness helps you identify areas for improvement and adjust your schedule accordingly.

- Single-Tasking: Resist the temptation to multitask. Instead, embrace the power of focused attention. Dedicate specific time slots to individual tasks, minimizing distractions and maximizing your introverted strength of concentration.

- Intentional Breaks: Schedule regular breaks throughout your day, seeking out quiet spaces to recharge. Introverts often need these moments of solitude to maintain their energy and focus. Use these breaks for mindful activities like journaling, reading, or simply enjoying nature.

By integrating mindfulness into your time management routine, you cultivate a conscious approach to your day, ensuring you use your energy and attention in ways that align with your introverted needs and maximize your productivity.

2. Technology as Introverted Time Management Ally
Technology is often perceived as an extroverted tool, a relentless source of notifications and distractions. However, when used strategically, technology can become a powerful ally for introverted time management.

- Task Management Apps: Utilize tools like to-do lists and project management apps to organize your tasks and set clear priorities. This reduces mental clutter and frees up your introverted energy for focused work.

- Calendar Apps: Schedule your day with dedicated time slots for work, breaks, and personal time. This structure provides a framework for your day, preventing you from feeling overwhelmed and allowing you to plan for periods of solitude.

- Communication Tools: Leverage email and messaging platforms to communicate asynchronously. This allows you to respond on your own terms, avoiding the draining energy of constant back-and-forth conversations.

- Noise-Cancelling Headphones: Embrace technology that blocks out distractions, allowing you to focus on your tasks without being interrupted by external stimuli. This is especially valuable for introverts who require quiet environments for optimal productivity.

Technology is a tool, not a master. Use it strategically to complement your introverted strengths and create a time management system that works for you, not the other way around.

3. Structured Routines vs. Introverted Flexibility

Introverts often crave structure and predictability, but we also value flexibility and the ability to adjust our schedules to meet our energy levels. The key to successful time management lies in finding the sweet spot between these two needs.

- Create a Flexible Framework: Instead of rigid schedules, build flexible frameworks that provide structure while allowing for adjustments. Schedule core work times, but leave space for spontaneous bursts of productivity or unexpected quiet moments when you can focus deeply.

- Listen to Your Body: Pay attention to your natural energy rhythms. Are you a morning lark or a night owl? Schedule demanding tasks during your peak productivity times and leave lighter tasks for periods of lower energy.

- Beware of Over-Scheduling: Introverts need time to recharge. Don't pack your schedule with back-to-back commitments. Leave space for breaks, solitude, and activities that replenish your introverted energy.

- Embrace Change: Unexpected changes can be disruptive for introverts, but they can also be opportunities for growth. Be flexible and adaptable, allowing yourself to adjust your schedule when necessary without feeling guilty or unproductive.

By finding the balance between structure and flexibility, you create a time management system that supports your introverted needs and allows you to thrive, not just survive, in the busy world. It's about creating a system that honors your unique needs and preferences. Don't be afraid to break the mold – schedule working lunches in a quiet garden instead of a noisy cafeteria, take solo walks to process complex problems, or plan late-night brainstorming sessions when the extroverted world slumbers. Embrace your inherent strengths – your deep thinking, your focused attention, your need for solitude – and let them guide your path through the time maze.

Chapter 13: Balancing Personal and Professional Life

13.1 Addressing the Need for Downtime and Recharge

Imagine a battery perpetually charging, never allowed to drain. No matter how efficient it may be, eventually, it would sputter and fail. Introverts, much like that battery, thrive on cycles of energy expenditure and replenishment. We pour ourselves into pursuits, both personal and professional, but neglecting our need for downtime can lead to depletion, burnout, and a diminished sense of fulfillment.

Recognizing the Importance of Downtime and Self-Care

Just as muscles need rest to rebuild, introverts require regular periods of quiet and solitude to replenish their inner reserves. Failing to acknowledge this innate need can have detrimental consequences. Imagine a sculptor, consumed by the passion of their creation, neglecting sleep and sustenance. The quality of their work would diminish, their passion wane, and eventually, their chisel would fall from a weary hand. Similarly, neglecting introverted needs leads to diminished output, a dulled spark of creativity, and a profound sense of exhaustion.

Downtime are not luxuries, but necessities. They are not about shirking responsibility or indulging in frivolous pursuits, but about nurturing the very wellspring of our energy and purpose. By prioritizing periods of solitude, introspection, and activities that truly nourish our spirit, we become more effective professionals, more engaged partners, and ultimately, more fulfilled individuals.

Balancing Work Commitments with Personal Needs

Introverts often excel in fast-paced environments, our focused nature and meticulous attention to detail enabling us to excel in challenging roles. However, this very strength can become a double-edged sword. Our dedication can morph into overcommitment, our conscientiousness into a relentless internal drive that pushes us beyond our limits.

Striking a balance requires conscious effort and clear boundaries. Begin by honestly assessing your energy levels and workload. Identify tasks that drain you the most and delegate them whenever possible. Schedule regular breaks throughout your day, even if it's just a few minutes of quiet solitude to recharge. Learn to say no without guilt, recognizing that prioritizing your well-being is not selfishness, but an act of self-preservation that benefits both your personal and professional life.

Furthermore, establish clear boundaries between your work and personal space. Resist the temptation to check emails or work calls outside of designated hours. This creates a mental "firewall" that protects your precious downtime and allows you to truly disconnect and replenish. Remember, a rested and rejuvenated introvert is a far more productive and engaged one.

Incorporating Restorative Activities into Daily Routines

Downtime is not simply about passive rest; it's about actively engaging in activities that replenish your introverted spirit. This will vary depending on your individual preferences, but some general principles apply. Seek out activities that allow for solitude and introspection. Spend time in nature, lose yourself in a captivating book, engage in creative pursuits that bring you joy. Meditation, mindfulness practices, and journaling can also be powerful tools for introspective self-care.

Don't underestimate the power of small but consistent daily rituals. Start your day with a quiet coffee break, end it with a relaxing bath, or schedule a weekly solo outing to explore a museum or art gallery. These seemingly insignificant moments can accumulate into a potent source of recharge, ensuring you face the demands of daily life with renewed vigor and enthusiasm.

By embracing your introverted nature and incorporating these strategies into your daily life, you can achieve a fulfilling balance between professional success and personal fulfillment. You can thrive in the world without sacrificing your unique personality and recharge your introverted battery for a life filled with both accomplishment and inner peace. Listen to your body and mind, respect your introverted needs, and carve out space for those activities that truly nourish your spirit. By doing so, you unlock the full potential of your introverted strengths, creating a life that is fulfilling, successful, and uniquely your own.

13.2 Maintaining Success Without Sacrificing Well-Being

The pursuit of success, particularly for introverts navigating an extroverted world, can feel like a relentless, never-ending marathon. We navigate demanding careers, cultivate meaningful relationships, and strive for personal fulfillment, all while carefully guarding our precious internal reserves. Navigating this terrain without sacrificing our well-being, that's the true definition of introverted success. And achieving this equilibrium requires mastering the art of maintaining success without sacrificing well-being.

This is not a matter of compartmentalizing our lives – a sterile partition between "work" and "personal" that leaves us feeling fragmented and unfulfilled. Instead, it's about cultivating a holistic approach to success, one where personal well-being fuels our professional achievements and professional accomplishments enrich our personal lives.

The first step in maintaining this delicate balance is recognizing the silent, insidious threat of burnout. It creeps up on us, cloaked in the guise of dedication and ambition. Deadlines become personal emergencies, sleep becomes a luxury, and our social interactions dwindle to work-related exchanges. It's crucial to listen to our bodies and minds, to identify the subtle warning signs before they escalate into full-blown burnout.

What are these warning signs? They are not always the dramatic breakdowns often portrayed in media. For introverts, burnout can manifest subtly. Irritability over minor inconveniences, a creeping cynicism towards work, a reluctance to engage in once-loved hobbies – these are all potential red flags. Pay attention to your sleep patterns. Do you find yourself lying awake replaying conversations or worrying about upcoming deadlines? Do you wake up feeling less rejuvenated than rested? These are your body's way of whispering, "Slow down."

Listen to your body's language. When deadlines become burdens, social interactions drain your energy, and the spark of passion in your work dims, it's time to pause and replenish. Don't mistake this for laziness or a lack of commitment. It's a strategic retreat, a wise investment in your long-term success.

Heeding this whisper is not a sign of weakness; it's a display of strength and self-awareness. Addressing burnout proactively is far easier than battling its entrenched consequences. Take a mental health day, delegate tasks where possible, and prioritize activities that replenish your introverted energy – a solitary walk in nature, a quiet evening with a good book, a heartfelt conversation with a loved one. Remember, these are not indulgences, but investments in your future success.

Beyond addressing immediate burnout, nurturing your well-being requires proactive self-care practices. Treat your mental and physical health with the same level of dedication you bring to your career. Prioritize regular exercise, even if it's just a solitary walk or a gentle yoga session at home. Make sleep a non-negotiable priority, establishing a consistent sleep schedule and creating a relaxing bedtime routine.

Fuel your introverted nature with activities that replenish your mental energy. Set aside time for solitude, whether it's a daily hour of silent reading or a weekend retreat to a quiet cabin. Connect with loved ones in meaningful ways, even if it means opting for small, intimate gatherings over loud parties. And don't underestimate the power of saying no. Learning to decline requests or delegate tasks is not selfish, but essential for preserving your precious energy reserves.

True success is not defined by a single metric, but by a multi-dimensional factors woven from professional accomplishments, personal fulfillment, and well-being. Celebrate the integration of these aspects, recognizing that your personal growth fuels your professional achievements and your professional accomplishments enrich your personal life. Don't be afraid to bring your authentic self to your work, whether it's your preference for deep, focused work or your need for quiet periods of reflection. Let your introverted strengths, such as your exceptional listening skills, your thoughtful analysis, and your unwavering dedication, shine through.

This steps of balancing personal and professional life is not always easy, but it is undeniably rewarding. As introverts, we may navigate a world that often misunderstands our needs, but within us lies a unique reservoir of strength, resilience, and creativity.

So, dear introverted friend, as you navigate the path to success, remember this: your well-being is not antithetical to your achievements, but rather the very ground from which they blossom. Nurture your mind, body, and spirit. Embrace the quiet power of introspection. And celebrate the calls of your personal and professional triumphs, knowing that your unique introverted steps is a testament to the strength, resilience, and undeniable value you bring to the world.

This is not just a guide to success; it's a call to redefine it. It's a declaration that success is not measured in accolades alone, but in the richness of your life, the depth of your well-being, and the joy you find in the delicate balance from both your personal and professional pursuits. So, go forth, introverted friend, and conquer not just the world, but the delicate balance within. For in that balance lies the true key to unlocking your greatest potential.

Epilogue: Beyond Success, Embracing Being

The book is closed, the final ink dried, yet the story it represents has only just begun. For this guide is not an end, but a compass, an invitation to step out of the shadows and onto the path carved by your own introverted essence. We have explored the intricacies of navigating success on your terms, of wielding your quiet strengths as powerful tools, of building a life that resonates with your values and fuels your spirit. But as we reach the final page, I invite you to turn your gaze inward, beyond the horizon of external achievements, and discover the true revolution that awaits: the revolution of simply being.

Forget for a moment the accolades, the promotions, the accolades showered upon you by a world enamored with extroverted displays. Let go of the societal pressure to conform, to mold yourself into a caricature of success defined by noise and constant engagement. Instead, step into the stillness, the sacred space of your introverted world. Here, in the quiet corners of your soul, lies a revolution simmering, waiting to erupt.

This revolution is not a battle cry against the extroverted world; it is a gentle uprising from within. It is a reclaiming of your natural rhythm, a celebration of your thoughtful gaze, a reverence for the power of deep listening and deliberate action. It is a turning away from the relentless pursuit of external validation and turning towards the nourishment of your inner landscape.

Imagine a garden, not a manicured display of vibrant blooms, but a tranquil sanctuary where delicate wildflowers peek shyly through the undergrowth. Moss carpets the stones, whispering secrets of ancient stillness. This garden, with its unassuming beauty, thrives not in the glare of the sun, but in the dappled light that filters through the leaves. This is your introverted garden, a space where authenticity flourishes, where introspection cultivates wisdom, and where quiet contemplation yields insights often missed by the rushing crowd.

Within this garden, you are not merely successful; you are whole. You are not just a cog in the machine; you are an artist carving your own masterpiece, brick by introspective brick. Your success is not measured in decibels, but in the depth of your connections, the impact of your thoughtful contributions, the legacy you leave in the hearts of those who truly understand you.

The introverted revolution is not about denying your ambition; it is about aligning it with your values, your energy, your unique way of navigating the world. It is about setting goals that resonate with your inner compass, pursuing them with the deliberate pace of a seasoned strategist, and celebrating your milestones, not with fanfare, but with a quiet sense of satisfaction that echoes in the stillness of your being.

Remember, there is no script for this revolution, no blueprint for introverted success. Your path is yours to pave, brick by introspective brick. Listen to your intuition, your gut instinct, the quiet voice that whispers wisdom from the depths of your introverted soul. Allow your strengths to guide you: your keen observation, your analytical mind, your capacity for deep empathy. These are not mere traits; they are superpowers waiting to be unleashed.

As you embark on this revolution, remember that your voice, though soft, has the power to move mountains. Your insights, though carefully considered, can illuminate the path for others. Your quiet presence, a sanctuary for those seeking refuge from the storm. Do not underestimate the ripple effect of your introverted being; it can reshape the very landscape of what it means to be successful, to be human.

This is not the end of the story; it is the beginning. The ink may have dried, but the story continues in the quiet moments of your life, in the choices you make, in the way you choose to be. Go forth, gentle revolutionary, and paint your own masterpiece. Embrace the quiet power of your introversion, and let your success story unfold, not with a bang, but with a ripple of purpose, a symphony of authenticity, a revolution of simply being.

The world needs your introverted light, not dimmed, but shining brightly from within. Go forth, and be the revolution.